D0112234

I HATE
DEMOCRATS

I HATE
REPUBLICANS

BY TIM YOUNG

Post Hill
PRESS

TIM YOUNG

I HATE DEMOCRATS

WHAT IF EVERYONE WAS WRONG?
AND I SAY WHAT IF, BECAUSE THEY ARE.

A POST HILL PRESS BOOK
ISBN: 978-1-64293-106-8
ISBN (eBook): 978-1-64293-107-5

I Hate Democrats / I Hate Republicans
© 2018 by Tim Young
All Rights Reserved

Cover art by Cody Corcoran

Post Hill Press
New York • Nashville
posthillpress.com

Published in the United States of America

After the initial manuscript was written I sent it off to a legal buddy of mine.

This is our conversation, that you should all read before you go any further.

Legal: Hey, so I reviewed the book. Do you have a few minutes?

Tim: Sure. What's up?

Legal: I get it. Funny, frank, etc., but it seems like you hate women and fat people. Mainly fat people and you're mean about it.

Tim: I am?

Legal: Yes.

Tim: You realize that the book is called I Hate Democrats, I Hate Republicans...soooo did you think it was going to be rainbows and cupcakes?

Legal: Okay, I get that, but you mention potential exes and you might be able to identify people from your descriptions, which could cause legal issues.

Legal: You don't directly name anyone but there are some pretty serious descriptions.

Tim: Well, if someone thinks that it's about them: All characters and events in this book—even those based on real people—are entirely fictional. All celebrity voices are impersonated...poorly. The following book contains coarse language and due to its content it should not be viewed by anyone.

Legal: Did you just copy the disclaimer from the beginning of South Park and change program to book?

Tim: Yes...and it works.

Legal: You have to put that in the book.

Tim: I'm literally just going to copy our entire conversation and put it in the book.

Legal: You're lazy.

Tim: You're annoying.

Legal: Okay, that doesn't cover hating women or fat people.

Tim: FFS. Let's see if I can cover this in one text.

Tim: I don't actually hate anyone based off of any demographics or things that they can't change about themselves. I don't hate women; I don't hate or dislike any marginalized group. I actually love people and America. I'm glad people are able to marry who they want and pursue their dreams. I disavow racism of any kind...including any hate group or individual who hates someone because of their race, color, creed, sexual orientation, religion...you name it. It's disgusting to hate people for any of that stuff.

Tim: You know what else I hate? That I have to clarify that I don't hate people because someone might take hyperbole or a line out of context from my book in order to frame me in a light that isn't true.

Legal: But you're harsh in the book.

Tim: I'm direct. And I'm not sorry if that hurts feelings. I'm not racist, misogynist, homophobic, yadda yadda yadda. None of it. And people who legitimately are horrible people.

Legal: Can you print something like that in the book as a disclaimer?

Tim: As I said...I'm going to copy and paste this conversation. And for bonus points...and I mean this. The first 3 couples who both show proof of purchase of my book, regardless of race, gender, sex, creed, or religion, who want to get married? I'll officiate their wedding for free.

Tim: Now, did I miss any hate groups that I need to disavow and denounce and call hate groups? Just text it to me and I'll denounce them.

Legal: I would ask, but of course you're an ordained minister.

Tim: $35 online. I paid the extra and was given a doctorate in "space and time."

Legal: Of course you did.

Legal: Also, you didn't cover hating fat people.

Tim:

Legal: Is that YOU?

Tim: Yes. in 2000. I think I was also 2000 lbs then.

Legal: So you don't hate fat people,
you hate yourself?

Tim: Close. I just hate people who don't take
personal responsibility and complain about it...
but THAT IS WRITTEN IN THE BOOK. WHICH
YOU SHOULD PROBABLY READ.

Tim: And this will be as well.

Legal: I think that covers everything.
Are you really not going to write a separate
piece and actually just cut and paste this
conversation into the book?

Tim: Do I lie?

Legal: ☹

Tim: Do you need a safe space?

"Republicans are such wusses."
—My Mom

"Tim Young is totally right and hilarious and so hot."
—*Your Mom*

★ ★ ★

TABLE OF CONTENTS

★ ★ ★

COLD OPEN

January 21, 2017—Washington, D.C.—7 AM

"I woke up early on a Saturday for this?" I mumbled to myself as I threw on a plaid blazer and headed out to the National Mall. "No one is going to be here." I live about a mile from the Mall, so I figured I would walk to perform my typical trolling of a protest. There would be a few dumb people with a few signs and it would be a light day. The camera crew I was working with thought the same and they casually, and probably drunkenly, showed up as well from the other side of the Mall from me; we would meet somewhere in the middle and take it from there.

At the point where I started, there was no one, but with every few steps I took, I saw more…more pink hats, more signs about literally anything and everything anti-Republican…and more mess.

By the time I reached the Mall, not more than fifteen minutes after I had left, I realized I was in a sea of thousands of women and the men they dragged with them. I was engulfed in a sea of smells from every possible person upset the Trump presidency had begun. It ranged from armpits to Avon, weed to desperation.

The attendees were a flowchart of the negative stages of grief: they ranged from anti-capitalists in denial of the electoral college yelling about how Hillary won the popular vote to depressed grandmothers dressed as very anatomically correct vaginas to angry liberal professors yelling about how this was the end of women's rights as we know it. No one there was ready for bargaining or acceptance…and in fact, to this day most of them aren't.

I barely had a moment to take in my surroundings when my phone rang. It was the camera crew across the mall; they couldn't find a hole in the crowd to get through to me and were stuck three hundred yards away. It was shoulder to shoulder and everywhere you looked were pink hats. It turned out a lot more people had non-refundable plane tickets and hotel rooms for Hillary's inauguration than I had originally thought.

Finally, a colleague who I was to film with that day was able to reach me in a strange open piece of the audience near the C-SPAN truck. "We're really fucked," she yelled over the crowd to me. Without hesitation, someone from the crowd yelled back "You know it, sister!" Her response was a lazy fist in the air. "How are we going to get out of this mess?" she asked me.

"I have a plan, but before we do, let's just take this in," I with a smirk, "plus, you're a woman. These are your people fighting for your rights that Trump is going to take away…he's going to take away *all of your rights*." Just as I said that, a woman walked by handing out American flag headscarves for women to show solidarity with Muslim women who choose or are forced to wear hijabs. I grabbed one and threw it on my colleague's face. "Here, be more modest and cover yourself up. You're distracting to the men who are here to fight for your rights." The irony wasn't lost on her as it seemed to be on the thousands of others in attendance.

Looking around, we spotted everything from the typical "Trump is orange" and "Not my president" signs to the more in depth three-dimensional bloody tampon puppets that looked like Muppets that were put in the 'do not use' pile from a failed middle school sex-ed curriculum. And of course there were vagina costumes and drawings…tons of them. Enough vaginas to make you never want to look at another vagina again. Enough vaginas that like…have you ever written a word so many times that you start to think it's spelled incorrectly even though it's the correct spelling? That's a good way to describe it. Even in a porn sense, standalone vaginas do nothing for anyone (as I'd imagine standalone penis pictures do nothing for anyone) so seeing someone dressed as one for a protest, then realizing there's a sea of them, was…gross.

There were so many women dressed as vaginas that after a few minutes, you could determine the economic means of the women wearing them by the quality. Were they hand-sewn? Were they bedazzled? Were they just facemasks or full-body vagina costumes? Could you identify the parts of them that men apparently have trouble finding when sex happens like it was some sort of biology class mascot? You get the point.

The rhetoric was just as ridiculous. Remember just a few months before, a bombshell was dropped on then candidate Trump when a decade-old tape of him speaking to Billy Bush of Access Hollywood was released and where he said,

"I better use some Tic Tacs just in case I start kissing her. You know, I'm automatically attracted to beautiful—I just start kissing them. It's like a magnet. Just kiss. I don't even wait. And when you're a star, they let you do it. You can do anything. Grab 'em by the pussy. You can do anything."

The public outrage was…not what the opposition to Trump thought it would be at the time. It only bothered people who already didn't like him, a pattern that continues to this day with his gaffs and shocks the political class. The attendees at this march? They were in the "still outraged" group…and are to this day. And they used that one quote, which to me sounds more like an elderly playboy trying to impress a young, hip television host than a man who sexually assaults women, to fuel what they now cheered for on stage.

Sure, what he said was disgusting, but when you use those lines to justify dressing like vaginas—and cheering for celebrities like Madonna who threatened literally bomb the White House, or the others who referenced graphic sex, violence, and swore on stage in front of children—you're literally no different. In fact, I would go as far as to say that I was in the middle of a rally that *loved* that Trump said what he said because it justified their ability to express the same low level of communication toward him en masse. In fact, thousands of women worshipped the line "pussy grabber," because it gave them the permission to be go to the same level. The signs quoting Michelle Obama's now famous line *"When they go low, we go high"* repeatedly being held directly next to those that said "Fuck Trump" exposed such a high level of obvious and in-your-face hypocrisy that you could easily begin to ignore it—and America, for the most part, has.

That day was eye opening to me. Because although I remember on election night in November being warned by my friend's wife not to celebrate Hillary's defeat in front of her, I thought she was in the minority of people behaving like babies because they had been handed the first presidential loss in the last decade. I was completely wrong. My eyes had opened up to a group of Americans that was taught that they could never lose and didn't know how to react when that inevitably happened.

After we finished taking photos and giggling to ourselves about the ridiculousness of the signage at the Women's March, we realized we were literally trapped—and not just trapped, stuck shoulder-to-shoulder in a prison of thousands of people in pink hats. How were we going to get out?

I looked around and locked eyes with an older woman in a wheelchair that looked as exasperated as I felt. I smartly squeezed my way over to her and asked her how she was feeling, when I already knew the answer. She couldn't see over the people who were surrounding her and just wanted to leave. She had gotten to the march by herself, but was immediately ignored by the ever-growing crowd around her as they clamored to hear celebrities talk about their menstrual cycles on stage. I asked her if she wanted to leave, to which she excitedly replied, "Yes, can you get me out of here?" Within moments, she agreed to go along with a cracked plan that I made and knew would work.

I called my colleague, who was now only twenty feet away, but also trapped in the sea of people and waited for her to get behind the woman in the wheelchair and myself. As soon as she arrived, I loudly announced, "My handicapped mother is sick and we needed to get her out to the other side of the Mall." The crowd of pink hats parted like the Red Sea, and we were able to get ourselves, that woman, and by the time we were finished, a train of about another ten wheelchair-bound women, out of the thick of the crowd of protestors who had forgotten and—in one case—even trampled them. Grateful, the handicapped women thanked me and my co-worker that we had escaped the human prison we were trapped in and had finally made it to the clear.

From the middle of Pennsylvania avenue, we turned around to acknowledge what we had just left: a mass of people who had forgotten what massive political loss looked like, many with an irrational fear brought on by campaign rhetoric that their freedom and their rights as Americans were about to be stripped from them. They had been fed the lines that if they lost the election, a fascist regime would sweep the land, that their freedom of speech would be squashed and worse yet, they might be imprisoned for their beliefs. Our American government is set up to stop any such regime and the elimination of rights from happening, but you couldn't convince a single member of this crowd that checks and balances would work. No, according to them, we were about to enter a time just before the fictional story of *The Handmaid's Tale*, where women would be objectified and forced to cover themselves because of an oppressive patriarchal religious regime who came to power...and they'd tell you that while voluntarily covering their heads with American flag scarves to show solidarity with those women who were part of a patriarchal faith that...wait a second...

Hit the music.... Wait. This is a book; I have to keep reminding myself of that. If this were a TV show, that was the cold open. We start at the Women's March right after inauguration, where there were hundreds of thousands of people worshiping the very words they decried foul coming from the mouth of Donald Trump, and where those same people had been led to believe that the end of their world was near. Now don't think that just one candidate or party got us to this point. It's both of them; it's the media; it's Hollywood; it's marketing; it's us.

People, we have a lot to talk about.

INTRO

★ ★ ★

BECAUSE EVERY BOOK HAS AN INTRO AND THAT LAST SECTION WAS ONLY THE COLD OPEN

We live in a divided America and it isn't going to change any time soon. We as Americans have been trained not necessarily to hate one another for our differing beliefs, but to believe that there are always heroes and villains, always underdogs fighting against "the man," and it's done us no favors.

What once could have been a serious and earnest debate has devolved into WWE's *Monday Night Raw*. We watch politicians and talking heads alike spout pre-scripted lines at each other for sound bites, clicks, and retweets so that they can cash in on low-hanging fruit without actually planning on changing anything. And we willingly tune in every day to our team's "home base" of a network to cheer on voices saying exactly what we think, to a chorus of easily defeated opposing voices.

In pro-wrestling, the heroes show off their strength by stomping out weak opponents or "jobbers" in matches that are of little significance other than to let the audience become familiar with the nuances of the wrestlers: their signature moves, their catch phrases, and their cool poses. You tune in to CNN to watch a weak conservative voice get railroaded by Ana Navarro or Don Lemon.

On Fox News, you watch Tucker Carlson stare blankly at whomever he disagrees with. It's all fantastic entertainment. Drop a hot news clip from the day for the first thirty seconds of a show and watch your favorites destroy the opposition for the remainder of the hour…but it shouldn't be interpreted as a way of life.

As a kid, or occasionally as an adult (who am I kidding? And as an adult), I became and continue to be a fan of Dwayne Johnson's character, The Rock. He had his signature moves, *The People's Elbow* and *The Rock Bottom* and his signature look, *The People's Eyebrow*, and when he spoke on the microphone, he had his catch phrase, "If you smell what The Rock is cookin.'"

I loved it. I watched it. I cheered it. But I also paid attention to the warning at the beginning of the programs he was on "Don't try this at home." To be honest, I probably paid more attention to the warning because I knew I'd look like more of a nerd than what I am if I went around yelling his catch phrase, but I also knew that he's a trained athlete and I shouldn't be trying to slam anyone around a ring. I've begun to believe that news programs and politics need a similar warning.

We watch our team defeat their opponents handily on national television in a redundant political theater, then we go out into the world and try to do it ourselves…and it typically doesn't work the way it does on television.

This is one of the many reasons why that as we've progressed as a nation, we as a people have become more equal, freer, and yet more resentful against our neighbors. We want to imitate the people we're fans of and even do what they tell us to do, but we aren't facing off against known entities that have been scheduled to lose to us. We're facing our very neighbors and Americans with whom we should ultimately be friends.

And why do you think we've been put in this position? Oh, I guess that's why you're reading this book. I'm supposed to pose these things as hypotheticals then give you the answer. Fine. It's power and money. We are all being manipulated for power and money.

Don't get excited about that last paragraph. No, I won't take this book completely off the rails into conspiracy land, although it wouldn't be hard to do. In fact, maybe check back in with me in forty years when I'm my conspiratorial grandfather's age. He believed we were being manipulated by the illuminati in some sort of ultimate, InfoWarsian power game. Life would be simpler if it were that easy. Unfortunately, it's not. There is no league of super-villains dressed as druids worshipping around an all-seeing golden eye…but while we're here, if that is a thing and I'm completely wrong, please send me an application to apply for membership. I'd make a great secret dictator.

Instead of illuminati, what we're ultimately faced with are two major political parties who have bills to pay and a government to try to be in control of and television networks that need to get eyes to watch them. Recently, we've seen offshoots of political parties get louder, because when you bet hard against your party and its winner (I'm looking at you #NeverTrumpers) you're really stuck between unemployment and absolute extinction. And those people get airtime because who better to cheer for than a "bad guy" who switched teams and turned good?

The magic of where we are isn't just that everyone is looking to pay their bills; it's that you have convinced yourself that you couldn't possibly be wrong. That's right—I'm looking right at you. In 2018 and the years just before it, the one thing that's been consistent is that it's always someone else's fault. Your job, your education, your housing, your interpretation of where you are in the world, and even your actions…the one link to all of it is you, but you'd never admit that. To admit that would show weakness.

When I talk about the failings of the Democratic Party in this book, you're going to love it if you're a Republican, but when I get to Republicans, you're going to groan and tell me that I'm wrong… or worse yet, tell me that I'm right, but a little off until it makes you angry and you tell me I'm wrong. The former is better because it wastes the least amount of both of our times. The same goes if you identify as a Democrat. Democrats will love when I say that the Republican Party has messed up big time on certain issues, but they might interrupt my dinner somewhere when they get to the part about how they can't get their acts together. The one link here is that it's easier to point fingers and blame at those who think a little differently than you rather than take personal responsibility.

What if I told you that the major issues of the day had no real policy solutions to correct for them? That we were yelling at the top of our lungs at our own echo chambers and throwing time and money at the leaders of those echo chambers to accomplish literally nothing. The fun gets kind of depressing doesn't it?

That's what this book is about. It's not about how one party is better than another; it's about how we all have failed, and how if we want to make our country great again, we're going to need to work together as a team—not just as Republicans or Democrats; not as progressives or conservatives; blacks or whites; Catholics or Mormons or Jews or Muslims; gay or straight; whatever gender against the other genders I can name (I don't know how many there are now anyway)—but one unified American team.

Now if you were triggered by that last paragraph, or even use the term "triggered" to define a state of emotion that someone puts you in, you might be beyond helping, because you certainly don't want to listen. To say you've been triggered, is to not take personal responsibility for your actions. I'm angry because you said or did something that offended me…as opposed to saying I'm angry because I took offense to what you said. That's where a lot of this book is going to go. Once we realize that we are the cause of our issues, we can work together to get things done. It's like the old saying that you can't love someone else until you love yourself… same concept. You have to take personal responsibility for your situation before you'll be ready to accept others.

So in sum: we all hate each other right now because we're being trained to do so by the media and political parties that aren't really putting up solutions to a lot of our issues. In addition to that, we aren't taking personal responsibility for our actions, which creates the perfect storm for a scenario where everyone yells at each other, gets offended by everything, and accomplishes absolutely nothing! Deep breath. That, my readers, is where we are as a country. So, if you're ready to take an in-depth and sarcastic look at how we're all stupid and getting worse, and you're willing to look in the mirror and point a finger right at yourself as one of the problems, then you've come to the right place. If you aren't ready, just leave me a 5-star review and call me a genius on Amazon.com before you throw this book in the trash.

CHAPTER 1:

★ ★ ★

A BRIEF AUTOBIOGRAPHY OF ME

Before we begin down the path of me telling you just how much you've been misled and you realizing just how stupid you may or may not be, it's important for me to lay the groundwork for you of who exactly the hell I think I am. And I know what you're saying to yourself. I came here to hate on things with you...so dance, monkey, dance...but you're going to thank me. After all, you inevitably need to know how to mock me when you get angry with me while reading...and trust me, you will get angry.

As I said earlier, at some point, something that I say about your party will make you take offense and say, "that's not right, F this guy," but you'll keep reading. I say take offense, because I'm not trying to offend you, but in the era of manufactured outrage and entertainment, you'll internalize something that I say and get testy. The first strike will be a simple F-bomb, but the second time you take offense...and surely there will be a second time... you'll be looking for some demographics to yell to describe me like you do at other people you're frustrated at when you're driving. Yes, you, me, and Jesus (or whichever deity you believe in) are fully aware that you get racist when someone cuts you off. I don't, but *you* do. This chapter is to give you some background to yell at me when things head south, or just to understand where I'm coming from.

For all intents and purposes, I really shouldn't be a Republican, but that's what I've been registered as since I first signed up to vote, and I'm sticking with it.

I was born in southwest Baltimore to a union pipefitter and an administrative assistant. I grew up in a middle-class neighborhood. My family was primarily middle class, yet frequently switched to lower-middle class when my father's union would argue something stupid and he'd find himself out of work for weeks to months at a time, but we made it work. Had it not been for my church community growing up, we probably wouldn't have been able to eat some weeks during that time period, but we never went without a meal. I never really discussed this with my parents, but I was an observant little kid, so I knew what was going on.

I was identified as really smart in elementary school, and the county, realizing they should cultivate smarter kids, brought a math tutor in to teach me advanced stuff that the other kids were identified as too dumb to learn. From there I was accepted into gifted programs in middle school and taken to a separate program at a farther away middle school than most of my friends. The middle school I got sent to had windows; theirs didn't. In fact, I'm pretty certain it still doesn't, but I've got better things to research at the moment.

Middle school is where I got involved in government: student government to be exact. I'm not exactly sure what a middle school student government accomplishes, but I signed up and ran for treasurer with no knowledge of money of any sort and I lost. This is where shit gets real. Not only did I lose—I lost to a kid who later in the year ended up getting busted for running an 8-ball drug ring in middle school. I lost to a middle school drug kingpin. Being in middle school government was a totally worthless bullet point without that part. I sometimes wonder what he's doing now… Drugs. He's probably doing drugs.

I stuck around in middle school SGA then kept up my effort in high school where I was in all the top classes again (I'm reinforcing this so you know just how smart I am.) And just in case you want to know how smart that was, I was valedictorian of my class. In addition to that, I was also student government president, National Honor Society president, stage director for certain shows, one of the lead trumpets in jazz band, and all sorts of other stuff that I don't remember. Basically, I did everything you could possibly do in high school that didn't involve athletics, because I was a fat nerd. Sure, all those personal milestones sound impressive, but to put it in perspective, when I graduated high school, I was told that the school itself was tops in the county in narcotics and teen pregnancy, and number 2 in dropout rate...so we just missed the triple crown of terrible scholastics. Additionally, my senior class president (different from SGA) was suffering from chronic depression (I hope they're well now) and we had a couple of kids with serious drug problems. We were a school full of winners in one of the poorest neighborhoods in Baltimore County, Maryland, but hey, I was the best of the pile. That was all in 1998. I think it's worse for kids in my hometown now.

After high school, I became the first person in my family's history to attend a university. Had it not been for scholarships, I was told that we wouldn't have been able to afford it. So when the first school came along that gave me a full ride, I immediately signed up. That school was the University of Maryland, Baltimore County (UMBC).

You might know UMBC as the first 16th seed team to upset a 1 seed in NCAA March Madness history, but before that, you had absolutely no clue was UMBC was.

I received what should have been a science scholarship that was dedicated to minorities and those who come from lower socio-economic classes to get into the science field, but I opted out of that deal for the easier-to-maintain-with-fewer-requirements general full scholarship. From there, I went on to the University of Baltimore, School of Law and then came back to UMBC to work on a doctorate that I never finished in public policy. At some point you get sick of people talking at you, especially academics who have more to say about themselves than the...wait...that's exactly what I'm doing now. I'll speed it up.

Where were we? That's right: I shouldn't be a Republican but here I am. Poor kid from one of the bluest cities in one of the bluest states, union parents, lots of academics…

Did I mention the fact that my first published article in a local newspaper was at the age of sixteen? From there, I worked in newspapers and journalism on the side ever since including the time when I decided to jump and take a crack at becoming a stand-up comedian. If that doesn't scream "biography of a progressive," then I don't know what does. But here I am, a republican.

I got involved in politics and immediately worked for Republicans. The majestic story that I tell political people is that I first voted Republican when I was in pre-school. At four years old, I voted for Ronald Reagan over Walter Mondale by picking a yellow square up with Ronald Reagan's face on it and putting it into a box inside a makeshift mini-voting booth. Reagan won the election fourteen to eight or something like that, but more importantly, I voted, and voted Republican for the first time in my life. Sounds amazing, right? It's literally a meaningless story about a kid who picked a face he had no clue about other than what he heard in his own household and voted, but it sounds so sexy.

From that point on, I would cheer on Republican candidates. I didn't know why. Heck, my parents didn't even know why, but I did. In 1988, I was excited watching the news with my parents, as George H.W. Bush became president of the United States. In 1992, I cried, yes, I cried like a nerd as my team lost and Bill Clinton was elected to office. That's not an exaggeration and don't think there was some deep political logic behind it. I was bawling my eyes out on the couch in my parents' living room when they announced Bill Clinton won. I can only imagine what they thought of their little nerdy fat kid when they watched him ball up and cry at the loss of the presidency by the Republicans.

In 1996, I didn't cry, because as a teenager, I could see how lame the great Senator Bob Dole looked against President Clinton. I thought to myself, "Why is this our guy?! It makes no sense." And I expected our team to lose, so it wasn't so traumatic. 2000 was a different story. I went to vote the day of the election and didn't realize that you had to register to vote before you just walked up to the polls. The genius kid that I described to you earlier here just wasn't so bright after all.

That was such a tough lesson and I made sure to register pretty soon thereafter so that mistake wouldn't happen again. I'd love to lie and say that I voted and was a champion of the George W. Bush's win so then you could blame me for the war in Iraq, but in my excitement about the GOP finally putting an end to the Clinton years I forgot to register to vote.

I did help distribute signs and volunteer doing little things around town for Republicans, but that was it. I made sure to work double-time for W in 2004. I felt like the lone Republican in my law school, so I made sure to put my knowledge and abilities to good use. First, I voted in 2004, let's get that out of the way, but I volunteered in what I was told was a "bad part" of Philadelphia as a member of the Bush/Cheney legal team. I actually bought one of the illogical "Vote or Die," shirts so I would blend better there and—get this—it worked. Apparently, a few members of the "Texas Strike Force," a terrible name for a legal team in the hood, showed up to a polling place, cowboy hats a-blazin', and had a gun pulled on them. Not shocking.

I worked my butt off for the Republican Party when I could and tried my best to stay involved and get people motivated for the party as well, but that's hard to do in Maryland. It's triply as hard to stay motivated in a young Republicans organization in said state where one of the leaders is an adult woman who has a collection of Barbie dolls that she claims look like her (like a serial killer would) and *also* a wall full of lizards in terrariums (like a serial killer would).

Oh, so why the hell am I a Republican? It's not a religious thing, or a disliking the other team thing...it's because the one common thread in all of these stories is that I learned the hard way that when the deck is stacked against you, you have to do everything on your own...aka take personal responsibility. I believe in hand-ups and not handouts, and that's what ultimately made my political party decision.

When my dad was laid off or on strike, sure he was forced to take up a sign and walk with his union occasionally, but he also immediately started looking for another job. He didn't like the idea of not working. He didn't want us to live off the system, because as he would say, "There are people worse off than us that need that money more than us." I learned that that you could do anything, get anywhere, and be successful with a lot of hard work and a loving family. And that's it. That's what made me choose my political team.

So I don't understand why there need to be more and more handouts in America. I don't get why the government should be there to take care of us, especially when you can do anything and achieve anything on your own and when in taking care of us, they slip in regulations telling us how to live our lives. People who believed that same way built this country, and it worked. It worked for hundreds of years, but then to win elections, we started to shift away from that and started creating programs that essentially gave handouts to people so that they would in turn vote for the ruling party. I can't say I fault Democrats for starting to do this; heck, it worked,but at what cost?

I watched as Obamacare passed and my team Monday morning quarterbackd in order to try to stop what should have been stopped initially. Then I watched them promise for seven years that they would repeal and replace it, only to drop that ball when they were in power. I watched Republicans repeatedly lose elections because they don't fight as hard as they could should or they don't vet their candidates, allowing crazy people get through to a national level.

But who's fault is it that this is happening? Can we blame party leadership? Can we blame the candidates themselves? The answer is no and no. Who to blame is us, me and you. It's our fault that these people get through and it's our fault that we aren't fighting the way we should. And by *our*, I'm not just talking about Republicans here; I'm talking about all of America.

"That can't be!" or "Yeah right, I can't wait to see what he has to say about this," is more than likely what you just said, but I bet right now you think you're a regular know-it-all. I bet you think you make informed voting decisions and really make a difference in your nation and your life. I bet you also think you're better than me because I forgot to register to vote in 2000. Well, you've got me on the registering to vote thing, but on the others, you would be completely wrong.

No one's above being stupid. Not even me.

CHAPTER 2:

★ ★ ★

POLITICS SUCK

Politics suck.

I don't know why you're interested in them. Forget all that stuff about rights and believing in America and yada yada yada... They'll just make you frustrated.

There are 3 types of people who love politics: nerds; people who want to rule the world; and our parents. No one else.

Odds are you're one of the nerds who are interested in politics. I'm kind of in-between a nerd and someone who wants to rule the world. It doesn't take a genius to realize that you or anyone else involved in politics falls into one or more of those categories, but what it does take is honesty.

Let's cover the simplest category of politics lovers first: nerds. They're going to be your political staffer that is completely enamored with their politician/boss. They're also going to be your media members who can't get enough of boring political rhetoric and love watching the same speeches over and over again just in the hopes that there will be a screw-up, like watching a NASCAR race and hoping for an accident.

Have you ever had the pleasure of getting to hear how important a political staffer is from that staffer? I wouldn't wish that conversation on my enemies. I think I'm a magnet for them. Don't get me wrong, there are a lot of wonderful staff members out there, but for some reason, the blowhards love to tell their life stories to me. They act like they're best friends with their boss and complain when their boss isn't ranked high enough. They talk about how they met so-and-so and one time saw Bono walk down the hall of their office building. This rant will typically go on for a while until I ask them what they do for a living:

They update Twitter…there are staff members who get paid to update Twitter.

I'm personally not impressed by anyone's political stories because mine are way better. I was on the Capitol subway—you know, that special private subway that only members and staff can take from the Senate offices to the Capitol—for the State of the Union address a few years ago with Senator Scott Brown and his wife. And get this, they were *totally* (picture me eye rolling here) making out. His wife turned to him and asked, "Do we really have to go to this," and he replied, "It's the State of the Union, so yes." Ok, maybe that wasn't a great story, but I've impressed quite a few people who are boring with it, so pretend it was better than what it was, will ya?

Oh, did I mention that I personally fall into both the nerd and the person who wants to take over the world? You would've figured it out eventually anyway.

To clarify: I've never really been a big fan of any politician, but I certainly have been guilty of watching multiple stump speeches in a row just hoping for a mistake or some sort of odd interaction with a heckler. Nuggets like the time that the head of a news organization interrupted one of President Obama's speeches when her duck quacking ringtone went off at the White House and he actually stopped to call her out on it. I don't necessarily live for that kind of stuff, but it helps feed my addiction. Also, you gotta laugh when Trump calls out a heckler…it's never not entertaining.

Then there's the media. First of all, let me mention that I love the media, especially those who are putting me on their programs or reviewing this book. Without them, the world wouldn't go around. If you identify yourself as a journalist or a media person and are currently reading, just skip the next few paragraphs. Don't worry; they are *really* boring and are completely worthless gibberish about nothing (aka what the reviews of this tome are going to be after you're finished anyway).

Are they gone? Good.

For the most part, political journalists are wannabe politicians, but know they'd never make it. Another big chunk are literally leftovers from beauty pageants. Both groups look up to the politicians that they love and they spin their stories that way. Shocked? I'm not.

Attention journalists: please also skip the chapter that covers the media...totally boring stuff you won't want to read anyway.

Gone again? Great.

I was Young Member Chair at the National Press Club for a little over a year, and what I learned first-hand during my time there was pretty disappointing. Journalists for the most part aren't non-biased. They kiss the butts of politicos they love and spin everything against those they don't. That goes for every age range and every publication and network.

This is a picture of myself as Young Member Chair of the National Press Club with the late Helen Thomas as we were jokingly going through the Playboy magazine in which she was the monthly interview subject. (Photo: Craig Hudson)

Don't get me wrong: there are great investigative and political journalists out there who make a difference and are amazing at what they do. They stand up for what's right and really focus on bringing information to the general public. But that's not the majority of them.

Hanging out with most journalists is like sitting at the nerd table at lunch in high school, and I know, because I was practically assigned to the nerd table in high school.

They're dense and just want what little attention that the cool kids give them. The bad part is that while Republicans are busy calling these nerds out on their spinning news against them, the Democrats are busy hanging out with them, making them feel good when they really don't care, and winning the media manipulation war.

Wait, there's a media manipulation war out there? Yes, Republican friends, there is, and we've basically lost it other than talk radio and Fox News.

Also, side note: don't ever date a journalist. Good or bad, they are so self-important and boring!

Journalists can begin reading again here!

So like I said, I respect every single journalist that I've ever encountered. I love their work and realize how incredibly difficult it is to be a journalist. So much hard work to really bring truth to difficult subject matters such as politics. With a tear in my eye, I say, "God bless you all!"

What about those people who want to rule the world? If you ask me, I'm more than likely talking about your favorite politician. If you asked me if I was talking about your favorite politician, you'd probably vehemently disagree.

Yes, people run for political office because they believe in America and want to make a difference in their communities. But let's face it, a lot of us can make that same difference without having to sucker people into giving us millions of dollars to pay for signs and staff to annoy people with.

At the end of the day, why do you want to be in office? Because you want power. And odds are, for most of the people who run for office, good or bad, if they kept getting handed higher and higher authority, they'd take it. Why? Because in the end, they want to rule the world.

Sure, there are a couple of altruistic people in the game, but they are few and far between. Senator Don Nickles from Oklahoma, whom I interned for on Capitol Hill, was one of them. He wasn't like the rest of the politicos that we see nowadays. Why? He could've kept getting re-elected and chose instead to go home and enjoy his life.

He was one of the youngest people ever elected to the US Senate and stayed for four terms. He could've easily, and when I say easily, I mean no one was going to even get close to him in polling, won a fifth term, but instead he chose to pack his bags and go home. He had served long enough and decided that while he was still "young," he should go and enjoy his family.

Not many elected officials at that level do that. No one in the US Senate does that. They stick around until their staffs are the ones talking for them and/or changing their diapers. They love that power and they wouldn't give it up for anything. Don Nickles probably could've been the Republican leader in the Senate; he could be enjoying what would be his sixth term by now, but he didn't stay. He was over it and he broke my mold of who loves politics.

He was different though, and I don't say that because I worked for him. I've hated many people that I've worked for, trust me. He was there to serve because he wanted to make a difference, but he just didn't love politics enough, so he packed up and went home to the home and family he loved more.

Most politicians out there who love politics are in it for life or until they die, whichever happens first. And again, if given the chance, you know they would totally rule the world.

There's something that helps prevent that though. See, way back on February 6, 1788, James Madison published *Federalist #51* and the single piece of theory that has kept this entire government together and functioning throughout its existence.

In it, he penned the line, "Ambition must be made to counteract ambition," which at its root keeps that second group of politics-loving people at bay.

At the end of the day, power-hungry people will fight other power-hungry people for all that power. They'll scratch and they'll claw; they'll pull out facts about others that turn into scandals; and they'll…I don't know, shut down government spending in order to get their way, and as far as I'm concerned, I'm cool with it.

We have a Constitution that was set up so that we would be able to shut down the government if we needed to stand up for what we believed in. Heck, we have a constitution that was set up so that we could physically fight the people who were in power if we *really* didn't like what was going on, so we shouldn't be too worried about non-essential programs being shut down.

Politicians know what they're getting into when they enter the fine world of politics. They know that with the evolution of media to what it is now, they're going to be under a microscope (especially if they're a Republican) so all this woe is me, garbage that we hear from people who want private lives when under a public microscope is just that: garbage.

Today more than ever, ambition is counteracting ambition and it's getting more and more personal, reaching into every aspect of everyone's lives. In the past three years alone, we've witnessed just how much people will scratch and claw to get over one another to get to the top.

I almost forgot about that final group of people: our parents. You know why they love politics? Because back in the day, they didn't have the internet, video games, and a trillion cable channels to distract them. Nope, they had a couple of TV shows, books, newspapers, and the right to vote. And you know what they did with it? They learned. They took the time to learn and focus and know what was making their world tick. They read multiple opinions from multiple publications and they formulated their own free thoughts.

All the previous generations had to entertain themselves with was information. Look at the history of the world.

When were complex math theorems and major discoveries created and found? In a time when there was no television! I often say that I'm sure that I would have created something meaningful to the world by now had I had no TV. Instead, I struggle to write a book while watching Youtube clips of *Family Feud* and wait for alerts on auctions I'm watching on Ebay. I'm also sitting in a busy coffee shop with some sort of terrible merengue music plays. You can make an excuse for everything in our time that's called the "Information Age" and call it information…or you can be real with yourself and call it what it really is: a distraction.

Back in the day, I would be sitting by candlelight with a pen and quill writing this stuff. And because it was a pain—if not impossible—to erase, I'd make damn sure that what I was writing was accurate and thought-provoking the first time I wrote it. Instead, I've got all that junk going on around me and I just deleted an entire paragraph because I didn't like how it sounded! This. friends, isn't an information age at all.

Our parents care because they are informed. And they were informed, God bless them, because they had nothing better to do.

Then there's was my mom. While she was alive, my mom was my Associated Press, even when I worked in media. She would call me any time something big happened in politics, even when I worked on the Hill in politics doing exactly what she would call me about.

Conversations would typically go something like this:

Mom: *"Did you see that anthrax scare?"*

Me: *"Yes, Mom; I was evacuated a while ago and now I'm back at my office."*

Mom: *"That was crazy, wasn't it? Did you see all those people evacuating the Capitol?"*

Me: *"Yup, they made us leave the building. It was really inconvenient."*

Mom: *"Oh, I think I saw you on Fox when they showed the clip. Are you wearing your blue tie today?"*

Me—*"Mom, everyone on Capitol Hill looks alike…white people in dark suits with blue ties."*

Mom: "Did you see that they're working on healthcare? What are you working on?"

Me: "Healthcare"

So that's it. Three different types of people love politics: nerds, people who want to rule the world, and my mom (and your parents too, but mainly my mom.)

EVERY STORY HAS AN ORIGIN OR SOMETHING

I am so tired of origin story movies. I skipped the first forty-five minutes of *Batman Begins* on DVD because I honestly didn't care about his whole training in the snow or whatever that section was about. It's boring. In fact I think the world, as a whole, is aware that if it's a DC Comics-based movie, it's not worth out time.

And as much as I love the David Craig *Bond,* I am starting to believe they're running out of ideas. The next step for the series is *James Bond: Paperwork* where we see the hero going through the dramatic application and required shots process for three hours.

We know that both political parties in America started somewhere, but for the most part, no one cares about their origins or the principles they were founded on—unless it's some sort of Democratic Party spin that they weren't the ones behind racism and trying to keep slavery. Sorry I didn't sugar coat that part. They like to claim that Republicans have shifted on all of their founding beliefs over the years when they really haven't.

Be honest with yourself: unless you're some sort of political nerd that lives and breathes the stuff, other than seeing an occasional EST 1860 or whatever date on a hat, you have no clue when the parties were founded and why.

Let's add some wrinkles to your brain while you read, shall we?

The Democratic Party is the oldest political party in the world...the world! And Nancy Pelosi was literally there to found it...or rather, she's been around for a long chunk of it.

They were led and basically created around 1824 at roughly the exact date and time when Andrew Jackson got pissed off about how the 1824 Presidential election was won. Political scientists declared this shift the beginning of an era known as the Second Party System. That's also around the same point in American history when stuff was getting so good on this continent that people had more time to care about politics and elections because we didn't have to worry as much about things like food, shelter, and being attacked by foreign entities. As it turns out, when you can fulfill your basic needs to stay alive, you can start to concentrate more on the economic and social policies of your land, which was still extremely far from where it is now. Before that, we were divided and we partied, but we didn't really divide the country up into political parties. Listen, not all the jokes in this thing are going to be winners.

The election of 1824 was comprised of four candidates that were all the same basic party: William Clay, Andrew Jackson, John Quincy Adams, and William Crawford. Adams won, and upon doing so, immediately named William Clay Secretary of State. This pissed Andrew Jackson off because he wanted a cool gig like that as a loser and he didn't get it. He accused Adams and Clay of colluding together to make this happen, so instead of everyone being equal in the race, it was really two versus one versus one, making the election a complete electoral mess, sending it to the House of Representatives where they handed the presidency over to Adams, the son of the former president who was magnificently played in a mini-series by that guy who also played the super villain Rhino in that terrible *Spiderman* movie.

Jackson started to immediately work on a plan so that this wouldn't happen in the future and created his own team of big-time candidates and notable folks of the day, including Martin Van Buren. Now I know you're saying to yourself, "So what? Martin Van Buren," but at the time, Van Buren was bald with huge tufts of hair coming out of both sides of his head and mutton chops kind of like Wolverine. So, he was pretty much the hottest hottie on the political free market (this fact may or may not be historically accurate.)

Jackson's team-up worked, and he rolled over Quincy Adams in 1828, naming that sexy pimp Van Buren Secretary of State. Van Buren, with his incredible locks, only grew in popularity and later ended up becoming president…but that's not part of this origin story. *Batman Begins* didn't have Robin, so this story doesn't need to talk about how Martin Van Buren was adopted after his family's freak circus accident…which also may or may not be historically accurate.

What was that, political nerds? You want to know why it's called the Democratic Party? There's actually a big debate among historians as to exactly why it's called that, and Ruth Bader Ginsburg won't tell us (I can make old lady jokes all day long), but let's just assume that that a pissed-off Andrew Jackson thought that elections should be more democratic and not electoral, because when the opposition has a better strategy than you and beats all of your hopes and dreams of becoming president with it, people start screaming about democracy and how life isn't fair. I'm sure he would have also blamed Russian collusion if he'd had the option.

Fun fact: the term "Democrats" was originally a derogatory term used toward well…Democrats. They didn't like the name initially as it was slang to knock them.

Democrats' main rival back in the day was the Whig Party. They were all about infrastructure improvements, like expanding roads (not fixing them because at this point we just needed new roads), deepening rivers, adding railroads, canals…you get it. They were on a roll too…up until the point when slavery was about to be extended into the new territories in the west thanks to the Kansas-Nebraska Act. A lot of Whigs and Democrats were all pro-business, and nothing helped business better than free slave labor, right? Except that around 1854, there was a growing group of people who realized that slaves were human beings and that it was disgusting to hold human beings as slaves.

Those people, the anti-slavery members of the Whigs and Democrats, came together that year and formed the Republican Party, a fringe third party that was named to support the "republic." So you see where that name comes from right there.

People were liking the idea of this new fresh third party idea and one of their hottest new recruits, a guy named Abraham Lincoln. And in 1860, roughly 150 years before he would be immortalized as a LEGO mini-figure, he was elected as a republican president of the United States. Only six years after this new third political party had started, their guy was elected president. That is one hell of a way to kick off a new political partywhich is I guess the exact same thing that happened with Democrats, but it took them two extra years to accomplish.

From that point on, the Republicans fought against slavery, eventually abolishing it and absolutely dominating American politics for the next seventy-two years. They did so well that they even made the former third party, the Whigs, vanish into thin air. Side note: could you imagine how depressing it must have been to be a member of the Whig Party that was on a great run in American politics and to have to show up to those last couple of meetings? I'd imagine you'd just drink, stare at a wall, and try not to cry when you get together…or exactly what fans do at New York Mets games.

Ever since then, there have been ups and downs, thousands upon thousands of people elected in the name of both…and sure, in the recent past, we've seen offshoots of political parties try to rise up and make a difference on their own, but essentially they get stomped out as well, due to lack of funding and only a fringe interest in what they offer. Take a moment and remember those we've lost: the Tea Party, Occupy Wallstreet, #NeverTrump, and soon, Democratic Socialists.

Does a book and a concept like the dislike of both political parties and their direction then become the prologue to a new third party? Tea Party 2: Electric Boogaloo or some other party that will pull members from both parties and change the world? No. Never.

Don't get excited. Quote me on this one: there will never be another successful third party. Not in our lifetimes and not unless there is some crazy revolution that is fought in this country…but if you think I'm leaning on the side of Civil War 2, please reference my chapter on fringe Republicans and Democrats called, "So You're Telling Me That There Are Crazy People on Both the Right and the Left?" Spoiler alert: Yes I am. And those are the only people who are ready to physically fight for our rights: whether or not they believe in heavier gun control laws.

So don't get excited. This book isn't about changing the world in radical or reactionary ways; it's about changing what's currently here…taking control of yourself and your environment and not looking too embarrassingly stupid when there are debates or people yelling at each other about politics in your Uber Pool…which makes literally no sense to do; we're all just trying to get across town together. I hate to ruin it for some of you, but we live in a democratic system with checks and balances that actually work. It just so happens that both parties are letting us down for one reason or another.

THE HYPNOTIST

You know how I took the time to tell you a little about me so that you can insult me when you get angry? Now it's time for me to tell you a little bit about you.

There are only two types of people in this world and it's not male and female, gay or straight, elite or not elite, privileged or not privileged, those at war or those at peace…or any two categories that have been shoved down our throats to divide us for the past few years. And I don't want to sound like someone with a "coexist" bumper sticker on my car, so I'm not going to say we're "all one people" and that "I don't see (insert any demographic)." We literally do see every demographic and color and when you say you don't, you're just lying to everyone.

The magic of the two types of people who I'm about to name is that you're definitely going to fall into one or the other group. You don't have a choice. It's who you are. And I absolutely discriminate based on these categories of people…in fact, everyone discriminates against these groups of people, at least one of them. You just do.

So who are these two types of people? They are either *dumb* or *not dumb*. Dumb and not dumb aren't determined by education, upbringing, social status, socio-economic class or anything else. I've met many a dumb academic. I've met many a dumb rich person or social elite. You can go through years of academia and training, work as hard as you can for your entire life, become extremely successful, and still end up dumb.

Conversely, you can have zero education, be completely broke, be given no breaks in life, and have no end to your struggle in sight and be not dumb. Let me explain.

The best way to break down the categories of people is by using the example of my friend who is a hypnotist. He actually took three total minutes to explain to me how to become a hypnotist, and if this political comedy thing doesn't work out, I would consider doing it for a living...that or stripping; it's really not that different of a profession.

Allow me to pull back the curtain to tell you how to be a hypnotist; it's very easy to do. All you have to do to be a hypnotist is dress, act, talk, and say things that are perceived to be what a stereotypical hypnotist does. Slick suit? Check. Calm, yet forcefully instructive voice? Check. A lot of short hypothetical phrases that shouldn't be questions but end up being questions because you put question marks at the end of them followed directly by affirmation? Check.

All that's left for you to do is show up to events that you label something deep, meaningless and yet digestible like "amaze" and get on stage with lights and maybe some music, and there you have it: you're a professional hypnotist. All that's left is your audience.

Most hypnotists start off their act with a trick to show you "the power of your mind." This trick involves clasping your hands together with your index fingers separate, pointing straight up in the air. You'll be told to relax but focus on your index fingers and when you do, you'll feel a force, similar to a magnetic force pulling them together. As you focus harder, you'll begin to realize that you can't control this force and when your fingers finally come together, you won't be able to separate them. Some 90 percent of the audience will not feel this force or have their fingers stuck together. But the other small percentage will be stuck, the force too great for them to break their hands apart. Those people will be asked to raise their now stuck hands in the air, and when they do, those dumb people in the audience will have revealed themselves to the hypnotist, who by the way is not dumb.

You see, when you clasp your hands together while pointing your index fingers in the air, your index fingers naturally pull together or lean in to each other. It's just how your muscles and ligament work. Try it now, you know you want to. I'll wait. There's no special magnetic force or power that pulls them together and there certainly isn't anything that keeps your fingers stuck together, but that won't stop people, even educated people, from falling for this trick. They are there to be entertained and they've been told that the hypnotist is, in fact, a hypnotist.

The hypnotist dressed, behaved, and talked exactly the way that the audience expected them to do. On top of that, the people who went to see the hypnotist made a decision to go to the show, purchased tickets, drove there, and intended to be entertained by the hypnotist. They even believed the man to be a hypnotist merely because he said he was a hypnotist. That's a lot of commitment. How, after all of that, could they be wrong? He clearly has special powers and abilities because he's there. Not only that, but look at your stuck fingers! Those fingers are stuck and there is nothing you can do about it.

The next step is go on stage, "sleep" when the hypnotist says sleep, cluck like a chicken when he tells you to cluck like a chicken, forget your name when he tells you to forget your name, or have an orgasm on stage because he tells you to have an orgasm on stage. These are literally the same "tricks" that every hypnotist performs and I'm not exactly sure why anyone would ever pay to see one.

I tell you how a hypnotist works for two reasons: one: my friend who was a hypnotist was a douchey asshole and I want his profession to die and two: to show you the two types of people that exist in the world, dumb and not dumb.

The hypnotist is not dumb. He has worked years to manipulate and make money off of crowds with this gimmick. The people who can be hypnotized…they're dumb. Really dumb. And if you're reading this and you've been hypnotized before, just lie to people from now on. Hypnosis isn't real; it's just the manipulation of dumb people into doing dumb stuff for other people's entertainment. And speaking of those other people who were entertained by the dumb people who were hypnotized, they are also not dumb.

Why ruin hypnotism? Why tell you about dumb and not dumb people? The answer is simple: it's no different than what happens in politics, entertainment, and the media surrounding it all.

Generically speaking, we have been trained to believe that people that dress a certain way, act a certain way, and speak a certain way are experts in their field. Additionally, we show up to rallies, donate hard-earned money, tune in to networks and want to believe in what's being thrown at us. That, just as I said about those attending a hypnotist's show, is a lot of commitment.

Unlike going to a hypnotist's show, however, you don't end up forgetting your name and having your fingers stuck together. Instead, you blindly listen along to talking points that have been created by a marketing and political team, or a group of producers who are just there to get ratings and make money. But you're not hypnotized, you're not dumb, you say to yourself. I bet for many of you, I could scroll through your Facebook or Twitter posts and see you coming to the defense of your favorite politician or bragging about how great your favorite news network's pundits were when they either did something incredibly wrong or merely stated facts that you already agree with and add nothing to our national conversation.

The problem with what I'm telling you here is that if you're dumb, which you may very well be, you'll automatically point a finger at someone you know who does this, but never look introspectively at yourself. It couldn't possibly be you. To test this, I'm going to take this time to drop two statements, both of which you will probably have a strong opinion about, but one you will most likely agree with and the other you will scoff at and put off onto other people. Ready?

1. Hillary Clinton broke the law and should be in jail for her illegal email server.

2. What Donald Trump said on the Access Hollywood tape was disgusting and implied that sexual assault of women was okay.

If you're a MAGA-hat-wearing Trump supporter, you'll cheer and 100 percent agree with the first statement, but then you'll call me a "libtard" when you get to the end of statement two. But, if you're #resisting so hard and believing in blue waves, then you'll have lots of excuses for statement one and want to hashtag #MeToo and declare me "woke" for the statement two. Both opinions show your bias and both show that you might…brace for impact…be dumb.

Face it, if you're like most Americans, you've committed a lot of time to politics over the past three years. Even if it's just watching on TV, voting, and believing in something, it's been a lot. You've put in hours of time discussing, absorbing information, discussing the topics, and celebrating or jeering depending on which side of the aisle you're on. You're going to have strong opinions on both of those statements either way…but very few of you will look at one and two and consider both to be accurate. Those who do see both in the same light are the not dumb ones. For the rest of you, I'd like you to try something for me. Clasp your hands together, index fingers in the air and try to resist the incredibly magnetic force pulling them together.

I believe both of the above statements that I wrote to be true. But I also believed both Hillary Clinton and Donald Trump to be viable candidates for president of the United States. How dare I, right? I was willing to accept the results of the of the 2016 election regardless who won. But a lot of you who are reading this would have been and are outraged.

So, what exactly got us to this point? Incredible marketing.

You see, the hypnotist doesn't have a crazy marketing strategy or billions of dollars behind him. And you'll rarely, if ever, see him pull his hypnosis shtick on television…mainly because no television host would fall for it, but in politics, there are entire industries based on just the marketing portion of the program.

Billions of dollars a year are put into the marketing of the political system in America to convince you that your favorite team and candidate are somehow connected to you…and more importantly, that you need them. You can't fault them for it, either. If you worked for something you believed in, you would want to do everything in your power to get as many people behind you as possible to help promote your ideas and leadership. The problem comes in when you're convinced that the candidate is a messiah or completely without fault, especially to the point that you're personally making excuses for their shortcomings, getting angry, and losing friends over it.

You have a life to live, rent to pay, and meals to put on the table. You have better things to do than sit around blindly defending someone who has a machine around them to defend them… that's what a dumb person would do. What's even worse is when the candidate that you favor does something so bad, so ridiculous that it's indefensible. As I write that statement, I realize that both sides of the aisle will think I'm talking about Trump, but I'm not. Don't be dumb.

Just because a politician wears a nice suit, gets on a stage, speaks in alliterative sentences. and wags their hand at the crowd without pointing (because psychologists say pointing is bad—that's why Bill Clinton never did it) and just because you gave up your time to come and hear them speak, bought a shirt, and really committed to them doesn't mean they're the end-all-be-all for what's happening in the world.

Similarly, just because a pundit or TV host does the same on your chosen echo chamber network, that doesn't mean they know what they're doing or talking about.

They are the hypnotists, you are the hypnotized. They are the not dumb people, and you, well we'll just need to work on it I guess.

I say all of that to say this. The people on your television and on stage are no better than you. It may actually be impossible to convince you otherwise because if you're reading this book, you've most likely put in significant amounts of time, money and effort into supporting and believing in someone and something that might ultimately suck. That's embarrassing, but we don't have to tell anyone about it.

There's even a good chance that you know more about specific issues—or all issues—than the people you are accustomed to watching on TV, but don't wait up for them to pull back the curtain and admit that; it would ruin their act.

One of the things I have learned throughout my career in politics, commentary, and comedy is to not be afraid to sit back, take a sip of a good bourbon, and admit that maybe, just maybe—and by "just maybe," I mean definitely—everyone has got it wrong.

CHAPTER 3:

★ ★ ★

NO ONE LIKES CONGRESS

While individual members of Congress poll well in their home districts and states, the whole of Congress can't seem to get an approval rating above 19 percent. This shouldn't shock you, as the legislature is easier to blame for the country's failings than the president himself.

At least when you poll people about their opinion of the president, you know that a large chunk of those polled will be for the man. After all, there are only two or three choices when it comes to for whom to vote for president, so odds are that the person being polled either voted for the current guy or against him. Nothing in between. It's a very black and white issue.

On the other hand, Americans can point fingers at around 432 members of Congress that they never voted for and who don't represent them when something goes wrong. Playing the simple numbers game, you can see why the people who occasionally go to work in the US Capitol will never collectively have a real chance of getting a high rating.

Simple logic aside, the people in Congress also haven't tended to agree on much lately (if ever) and at times really don't have policy solutions to many of the hot button issues that are plaguing us or that are front and center in the news.

Let's take one of the hottest issues of our time: gun control. As soon as a tragedy hits, social media and television news channels are flooded with opinions on whether or not Americans should have the right to carry guns, what types of guns they should carry, and who we should blame for the shootings.

I'm going to let you in on a big secret that no one says when a terrible and tragic shooting happens: there's no policy solution that could have stopped it.

Yes, I'll explain myself.

In the middle of the outrage blame game after a shooting, fingers are pointed everywhere but at the shooter. The NRA gets blamed, Republicans get blamed, gun manufacturers get blamed, television shows and video games get blamed...everyone gets blamed except the criminal that obtained the guns on their own and chose to commit their evil act on their own.

None of the organizations or entities that I mentioned that got blamed can possibly be responsible for one individual's actions. Limiting any of them would do nothing to stop the shooter. If a criminal wants to commit a crime, they will do so. If a psychopath wants to kill people, he will do so.

Sure, we could arm teachers and put more guards at schools, and sure, we could ban all guns...but that POS who wants to kill kids or innocent people by shooting them will find a way to commit that crime. Their brain doesn't work like ours. Laws won't stop them.

And even if we did ban all guns and eliminated them from the streets, what would happen next? For that, we only need to go to London, where they are having a record number of stabbings and knife attacks this year. They're one of the most violent cities in the world and to combat this...they are now considering "knife control."

There isn't a policy solution to stopping crazy people from killing others. There just isn't. Laws are already in place to deter people from doing it, and it doesn't stop them. Most of these people want to die themselves, so they don't care about the laws.

Why talk about guns here? Because Congress can't win on the issue...but they sure are loud about it.

Congress and our lawmakers know that people are rightfully upset about these senseless killing and want something to be done, so they scream and yell about it…but in the end, they as well as you should know that no policy passed will stop a psychopath from killing people if he wants to. I know that's incredibly dark, and I promise to get back to shit-talking about other things, but it had to be said.

Congress finds themselves in similar situations with other, not as dramatic policies too. Coupling that with 535 egos and 535 different platforms for different agendas, and that's what gets them stuck in place, accomplishing very little…and pissing everyone off—well 81 percent or more of people off in the process.

No one likes them…and as a whole, they just can't win.

CONGRATULATIONS, YOU'RE BORING

One of the major problems that Americans face is where to find an honest, unbiased news source. I'm honestly not sure where to look for one anymore, and rightfully so. To pretend that the echo chamber you tune in to or open up to read is telling you the full, unspun truth is simply that: pretending.

As I began with in an earlier chapter, calling any channel on your television a "news network" is a complete misnomer. There's no altruistic desire from the network to provide you news. They have bills to pay and need your eyes and ratings to pay them. Perhaps sometime in the not-too-distant past, the networks started with the concept of providing news to you in an unbiased and dry manner, but then things started to change…and they really started to change with Roger Ailes.

Sexual assault and harassment allegations aside, Ailes was the first guy in entertainment to know that news was as dry, boring and depressing as news is, so he mixed things up a bit. He literally was the guy who came up with the idea of moving chyrons and swooshy sounds and moving effects when you shift from story to story. It's been going on so long now that you probably can barely remember a time when we didn't have that. Once the sounds and movement on screen were a hit, he went into casting, he went full-on entertainment with it…the best of which can be seen on Fox News's *The Five*.

The Five, according to the Wikipedia page on it that references the initial press release, features a "roundtable ensemble of five rotating Fox personalities who[…]discuss, debate and at times debunk the hot news stories, controversies and issues of the day." But it's far more than that. You see, Ailes loved theater, so he booked *The Five* as the five top archetypes in all theatrical productions… and once you read this, you'll never be able to unsee it. There's the hero, the villain, the comic relief, the princess/damsel, and the professor/nerd. Don't believe me? Just look at the casting.

Originally, the hero was Eric Bolling. He's the anchor of the show in the middle. He even looks straight out of central casting like a guy who would send some dick pics to women…sorry I got lost; he did totally do that, but he looks like a tough hero type. To his right and our left was the villain, who for a while was Bob Beckel, but is now Juan Williams. They are the liberal on a show cast full of conservatives, and the last person that the home audience would ever agree with. Why would they want to watch this villain? To see them get defeated by the hero and the cast of the rest of the show.

To the hero's left and our right is the professor, or the most intellectual and experienced of the panel. In this case, it was one of my favorite Fox News personalities, Dana Perino. There is no doubt that Perino is a presidential and political veteran whose strength comes from her infallible demeanor and intellect. Ta-da! The professor.

Next to her on the far right side of the table to the audience is the comic relief of Greg Gutfeld, or a cast member from *The Greg Gutfeld Show*. Before they had to move quickly to replace Bolling, it would be Jesse Watters, but the other day I saw that it was Tyrus. All the same, they are there to play comic relief and take a bit of the edge off of serious discussions and they typically play that role perfectly.

And finally, on the far left of the screen to the viewing audience is the damsel or princess. On Fox News's former super late night program, *Red Eye*, they called this position, "The leg chair," because that's what it's there to do, show off legs like a 1980s ski school movie. It is always occupied by the most vampy and attractive of the panel, which is Kimberly Guilfoyle.

The Five is brilliantly cast, and the ensemble provides great television. Don't get me wrong. I'm not here to knock being entertained by networks; I'm just here to remind you that "news networks" aren't here to give you news so much as entertain you.

Other channels haven't quite caught on to what makes Fox News so successful and number one *all the time*. But what also might help the channel is the problem of supply and demand. There are multiple liberal leaning networks to watch, so you have choices there, but when it comes to conservative and right leaning programming that's labeled news, your only choice is basically Fox News.

The only fault I would give a network like Fox is that with practically no competition in the marketplace, there's no reason to innovate. They know what works for them, and there's literally no reason to try something out of the box or new.

On the other side of the aisle you have CNN and MSNBC, who…frankly aren't as entertaining when it comes to the presentation of news. CNN in particular started as an altruistic news source, but, like any good clickbait digital marketer would do, shifted to what was working for them, especially during the 2016 election cycle.

They even flat gave up on certain times of the week and added original—and quite entertaining—programming.

The more that the left and parts of the right became outraged by the candidacy of Donald Trump, the more sensational CNN would take their commentary…and I'm sure internally the executives liked what they were seeing and the audience numbers affirmed this shift. I can't blame them for it. If the numbers work for them, then so be it.

And MSNBC? MSNBC will run movies *like All The President's Men* on Sunday nights to save money and troll the president in a not-so-creative-or-good-for-ratings kind of way. They've essentially turned blocks of their network into three-hour long tweets.

In sum, there aren't unbiased media sources anymore. I could rant and rave about individual journalists, but it doesn't take a genius to know how they fall politically. If you don't get it from their spin on air or in their writings, just look at the tweets they like on Twitter. It pretty much shows where they lie politically. You can look at mine too. I'm sure I've liked all sorts of ridiculous stuff that isn't just "LOL" responses to my own tweets.

So where should you turn for honest news? Everywhere. It's the sum of all the opinions that can lead you to the actual truth. Take out all the spin and look at all of the news presentations on your own. Remember that news channels are only here to entertain you, some worse than others, and that the actual facts of what they're talking about over an hour or two hour period take up less than a half of a page of bullet points.

Be smart, but don't stop watching the shows you love to watch…and hate. They're both there for your entertainment. Or, ya know, go outside and enjoy your life after you realize what's actually going on in the news.

CHAPTER 4:

★ ★ ★

DEMOCRATS — THE ANNOYING EXES YOU TALK ABOUT AT PARTIES

Anyone with a level head gets the strategy of the left: make their president/presidential candidate seem cool and he can get away with anything.

It started with the JFK; it faltered with Jimmy Carter, but that was later recovered; it dominated with Bill Clinton; and it exceeded that domination with Barack Obama.

Fool America once, shame on you; fool America twice, shame on America; fool America numerous times,and we kind of deserve it at this point don't you think?

I'd prefer if we lived by George W. Bush's interpretation of the old adage

"Fool me, don't fool me again."

You would think that Americans would catch on at some point, but then again you would be making an error in thinking that Americans would be smart enough to understand how they were being tricked.

Let's start with JFK. What positive things did JFK accomplish in office? I did some intense research on the subject and came up with the following list:

1. He was the first Catholic elected president.

2. Marilyn Monroe…and apparently any woman that walked within five feet of him.

3. He was so cool and attractive.

If you ask any Democrat, JFK was one of the greatest presidents of all time. Why? He was so cool and attractive. Remember that? He was both cool…and attractive.

I left a few other things off of this intense list. He was a trendsetter and had a wife who was also incredibly fashionable and entertaining. They had beautiful kids and they lived a beautiful… wait a second, I'm saying the same superficial things over and over again, aren't I? That's because that's all that he accomplished that was positive: superficial things.

I love thrift store shopping and hunting at antique malls for cool stuff. Over the years, I've amassed a pretty solid collection of antique government documents for relatively nothing, so it's easy to understand that I love digging around for treasure at huge markets and old moldy-smelling shops. I see the pricing of stuff that's out there and let me tell you, anything Kennedy is *super* expensive. I saw just the auction book from the Kennedy estate sale after Jackie O. died. Just the book that showed pictures of the estate and base pricing on each item was selling for one thousand dollars!

One thousand dollars for pictures of your junk! And not like Eric Bolling/Anthony Weiner junk that they took pictures of (had to get that in there…that's what she said…I can go on all day long). Can you imagine? That's how cool they were. I just want to get to a point in my life where a book of pictures of my junk (stuff not penis) would sell for fifty dollars!

On a grand scale, Kennedy failed at most every policy he attempted to enact…but we don't never talk about it and for the most part, Americans don't stay continuously informed about that. On the other hand, there's Jimmy Carter.

He's what we would call in this context, "not so attractive" and as a peanut farmer from Georgia with his wife Rosalynn and daughter Amy, he didn't have that cool Northeastern/Hollywood charm that the Kennedy family brought. They were a hardworking family, rough around the edges...and if you're a hard worker who doesn't look all that hot and you fail, you're just out of luck.

Let's face facts: when you deal with a grungier, not as attractive president, you can't really divert attention away from his poor policies. Under Carter, the country tanked (just like today!), but he didn't have anything cool to fall back on and divert attention with.

The Democrats hadn't quite mastered the media like they have today. I mean Obama had top-level staff married to presidents and executives of networks.... He's *that* good! But old Farmer Jimmy and the DNC hadn't locked down the nepotism/marry into the family game quite yet, so he was stuck having to face facts in an election. Sucks to be him, right? Well, at least it sucked that he didn't have the spin that we have today. he Democrats threw him a big bone a few years ago to be nice though—or maybe to rub in their complete domination of the media, they made a movie to make him look awesome. Remember? He was the heroic punch line of *Argo*.

Not only did they make a movie to make him look awesome, but then that movie won Best Picture at the Academy Awards! And guess who announced the award for the Jimmy Carter propaganda film: Michelle Obama! I'm sure you saw *Argo*. It was a great movie, don't get me wrong, but I swore out loud at the end when I heard Jimmy Carter's voice describing how he wasn't able to speak about how successful he was with this program and you should have as well.

Yes, *Argo* from the get-go was a propaganda film talking about how smart and successful America was over Iran. I have no problems with that. In fact, we were, and go USA! We should be nationalistic and believe that we are better than other countries because we are. But when the movie took a turn toward loving Jimmy Carter and reminding us how great he was, I all but threw up my popcorn on myself in the theater. I realized that I had been duped into watching a big propaganda film to take credit away from Reagan and give a nod to the Democratic Party.

Shoot me in the face.

When I watched the Academy Awards live only because I was dating a woman who took me to an Academy Award party and not because I voluntarily wanted to watch it (ulterior motives make me not guilty), I knew what movie of the nominees was going to win as soon as I saw Michelle Obama's face appear to deliver the award. What business did the First Lady at the time have giving out awards at the ceremony? Well…unless that award has something to do with helping out the Democratic Party's cause, which was of course, making Jimmy Carter look like a million bucks… or five hundred million bucks or whatever number they made off of that movie.

If this same media machine were around in the 1970s, who knows? We may never have had Ronald Reagan as president. I know that's blasphemy for any Republican to even suggest that Ronald Reagan may not have ever existed, but think about it. Obama became untouchable in the media…we're going to get to that in a bit, but let's conclude the discussion of Jimmy Carter with this: I bet he wishes that Ben Affleck would've been around in 1979.

Oh, and the best part about this entire scenario: who called out the Obama administration and the Democrats for this absolute propaganda award and film? Not America. No, definitely not the American media, because they're all in support and awe of the movie and the presidency. That would make too much sense for them to have free thoughts.

Who called them out? An Iranian military group. General Mohammad Reza Naqdi, commander of Iran's Basij, forces gave Michelle Obama what they called the "wet gunpowder award," for showing that Hollywood was truly in the back pocket of the White House and the Democratic Party. According to Naqdi, "If we spent billions to show the truth about the Oscars to the world we wouldn't be able to do it, but this action from Obama's spouse showed the truth about the Oscar awards to the world."

Well, take note: this is probably the first and only time that I'll agree with a representative of the Iranian government. And I know he probably would hate me if we got together for coffee, but he's spot-on there.

He continued, "God showed America's hand, and a film that is cheap, without content and inartistic that they picked for an Oscar award caused them disgrace." Okay see, I agree that it wasn't really that artistic. They were just recounting a story, but other than that, this where he lost me. I paid fifteen dollars to see this in the fancy, leather recliner theater where you order food and they bring it to you, and I thought that it was a well-made film (up until the part where I heard Jimmy Carter's voice). I also don't think that it was cheap or without content. Add in the fact that I'm also certain that we worship different Gods and we're back to disagreeing, but don't fault me for trying to find equal ground General Naqdi. Maybe if he's also regularly let down by the New York Mets, he and I could be cool again.

Where was I? Oh yeah, talking about how we're told that Democrats are cool and sexy.

We couldn't get through this section without naming every Republican's favorite presidential super villain: Bill Clinton.

By the time George H.W. Bush was up for his second term, the Democrats had realized that they had do pull out every trick in the book to make sure that Clinton got into office. They needed demographics of people to vote that don't usually vote: black people and young people. And in order to get them to vote, they needed another sexy president that could reach both.

They had their man in Bill Clinton because he was smooth and calm under any bit of pressure, but more so than that, he could play the saxophone and would answer any stupid question that you would throw at him.

Forget what he did in Arkansas, ladies—or to the ladies in Arkansas—what type of underwear does he wear? Bill Clinton famously went on what was then a channel that played music videos all day long. It's called MTV, or Music Television. Now, it plays terrible teen drama and pushes stories about progressives who have been victimized by Trump through a news outlet that somehow covers things other than music. I digress.

Bill Clinton went on an MTV town hall to make him look awesome to young people and they asked him what type of underwear he wore.... Now, I don't know if you're aware of this or not, but questions are pre-screened at these "open forums," especially warm and welcoming open forums for progressives like that on MTV. So their goal was to make him look *super sexy* by talking about the underwear he wore. Gross.

I don't even remember what his response was, but just know these two things:

1. Hillary probably doesn't know the answer to that.

2. I'm boxer briefs, the perfect storm of comfort and stability. I want to know everything is there while my upper thighs are hugged by cotton. You're welcome.

Wait, there's more?! Yes, Bill Clinton went on *The Arsenio Hall Show* to play jazz music with his saxophone! What? He can play a traditionally African American dominated music genre moderately well on a late-night talk show aimed at the African American demographic? He's the perfect storm of cool and sexy!

The Democrats had done it!

Well, they sort of did it. Their success was because of their media mastery combined with the fact that George H.W. Bush was so removed from modern life that he was amused by the newfangled technology known as a price scanner at the "common-people's" supermarket. His looking at his watch during debates like he has somewhere better to be did him no favors.

Oh, and lest we forget, Ross Perot pulled fiscal conservatives away from Bush in that election with his constant barrage of flow charts. H.W. just didn't stand a chance at the end of the day. Side note to the younger crowd that have no idea who I'm talking about with Ross Perot: he was the O.G. billionaire outsider candidate who took a swing at running for office and he was known for buying up lots of national television time to show off piles of charts that he had printed up to run for office. Had he not run,

George H.W. Bush would have more than likely had a second term in office.

You see, the goal of Democrats, and really any political party is to spin their candidates in a better light than the other teams. When you can do that, you can literally rule the world. When Democrats do it, Republicans rarely or ineffectively rather call them out on their game. Instead of calling a duck "a duck," they sit back and take the spin, reacting to policy rather than saying, "Wait a second, that candidate sucks and you're trying to distract us with them appearing to be cool."

Clinton got away with that election, the next election, and a ton of garbage in the White House because he was spun to be cool. But what if he had effectively been called out? When's the last time a Republican candidate other than Donald Trump just stood up and said it takes a lot more than just being cool to run a country? That might be one of the reasons we have our current president. Because for years, Republicans would sit back and let their candidate, who in many instances had better policy ideas to protect our country and put money back into the people's pockets, take a whipping based on what has essentially become a popularity contest.

Fool America once, shame on you; fool America twice, shame on America; fool America over and over again, then shame on... Oh wait, we haven't even gotten to how cool Barack Obama is yet, have we?

Barack Obama was the perfect storm of cool and attractive. Add in the novelty that he's the first black president, and the GOP had absolutely no chance of defeating him after George W. Bush left office.

Did I mention that the president was black? Stop right there; I must be a racist. *Democrats got to tack on that excuse for not supporting Obama! What a win!*

The 2008 Obama campaign was run on a few major issues that you all are aware of:

1. He wasn't George W. Bush

2. He's so cool and attractive.

3. He could be the first black president.

That's it. He definitely wasn't running on experience. He was a community organizer from Chicago, which I'm still not quite sure what that means even years after the fact. Last week I asked a couple of my friends out for drinks and picked a bar, which I think qualifies me as a successful community organizer. He was then elected (or walked in) to a US Senate seat. From that Election Day on, he began running for president, literally with the above listed qualifications. He wouldn't even really show up for work on the Hill that much.

And for some reason, America has been tricked into dancing along with those three qualifications ever since. If you notice, they weren't far off from the accomplishments of JFK. If you're popular enough and you know how to deliver the lines, people, the gimmick sells. Even looking back on his legacy today, people still note that he was correcting for George W. Bush...the above three qualifications *are* what is listed as his legacy.

The first two years of the Obama presidency, Obama accomplished absolutely nothing...and Democrats had complete control of both the Senate and the House of Representatives. In theory, he could have basically done anything that he wanted, but he couldn't get anything done because he couldn't rein in his party and their egos enough to do so.

Give him some credit, though; he hadn't started signing executive orders like they were going out of style yet. He was too busy blaming W and Republicans in Congress and everyone else but himself.

In his first two years as president, the economy was tanking similar to what happened during Jimmy Carter's administration, and some of his worst numbers came in during the end of his first term, but you wouldn't have known that because Americans were shown over and over again how cool he was. He was on the cover of magazines, on every late-night talk show, and rarely if ever portrayed in a negative light by his friends in the media.

Then there were his opponents. The first one that he simply stepped over to become president was John McCain. My entire assessment of that election was, "I mean…come on. What did you think was going to happen?"

Then there was his second opponent, Mitt Romney.

I hate to break it to some of you die-ard Republicans out there, but your presidential candidates pre-Trump could be described at best as stiff, out of touch, and stodgy…regardless how much policy experience and knowledge they have. John McCain and Mitt Romney are people who really could have made a difference in the country in their times and carried the correct platform to vote for in each of their presidential elections, but in comparison to Barack Obama, they were, well…not as cool.

Sadly, when most Americans break down what they believe and where they stand politically, they agreed more with McCain and Romney than they did Obama, but when the rubber meets the road, people are going to vote for the package rather than the actual information.

My angry veteran grandpa doesn't beat the cool black guy in a popularity contest,

and Rich Uncle Pennybags who left his top hat, monocle, and cane at home doesn't beat the cool president of the United States in a popularity contest. Period.

Do I think this country would be in better shape right now if Mitt Romney had been elected president? Absolutely. Did I think he had a chance in hell of being elected? No. And it was literally because he wasn't as cool as Barack Obama. It's a sad state of affairs when Americans won't look at facts, but rather the package that they come in, but that's showbiz…I mean politics!

Even through today, Democrats have proven themselves to be the masters of political spin. They know how to pounce on issues and take away freedoms better than the Republicans do…. Like how I slipped that jab in there at the end?

CHAPTER 5:

★ ★ ★

REPUBLICANS — THAT TEAM THAT JUST COULDN'T SEEM TO MAKE A COMEBACK UNTIL AN OUTSIDER DID IT FOR THEM

Before I break into this section, I want to note that some of the thoughts in this book are essays that I had written nearly five years ago about the current political climate that had never been published. The interesting thing about this section is that I had predicted that a character like Trump was needed for the Republican Party to win again. Read this next part which was an original excerpt from me at the time and be as shocked as I was that the party seemed to have found their "hero supporting character," in who became their new leading man, Donald Trump.

Here we go:

"Comparing the GOP to the Democrats on strategy is something well, difficult to do."

What is the Republican Strategy?

Rather than focus on manipulating people or spinning things out of control, I think they basically believe that the truth will come out and that a big supporting character will expose the false rhetoric from the left. Sadly, politics isn't every other chick flick movie, there is no supporting character to help Kate Hudson win back the love of her life here by exposing the lies of the antagonist.

Without this hero, the GOP's strategy is disappointing to say the least…Okay, it sucks.

We're completely failing at not only counteracting the left, but at successfully reaching out to all minority groups and young people. How can that be?

I sat and watched on the sidelines while our presidential candidate Mitt Romney got stomped out by Barack Obama in the 2012 campaign. It was so bad that every time Romney would say something off key, there would be a commercial about it. We'd get smacked at every corner. Big Bird, the 47 percent, binders full of women…each and every time Romney said something wrong, the left was down his throat. And what did we do to counteract it? It seemed like nothing.

Side note: Ain't nothin' wrong with having binders full of women.

Side note 2: If you're single or something.

I no longer would get phone calls from my mother asking what I did that day or what was in the news, but rather calls where she would lead not with hello but, "My God, Republicans are such wusses! Why won't they stand up for themselves?" And that's exactly what I was thinking.

Maybe it's who we have working for us. I mean, Mitt Romney was a great guy and someone who loved this country, but he looked like the epitome of a white male Republican president… or Mr. Fantastic from the *Fantastic Four,* kind of a toss-up in my mind. So when he stood up against Barack Obama, he looks stiff, stodgy, and like everything that Barack Obama wasn't.

The problem was that he was everything that Obama wasn't in a good way. He understood how the economy worked and since he was already so wealthy, really didn't have any interests in anything other than helping out our nation as president.

The left would stomp him down for running Bain Capital and becoming a billionaire or however much he's worth, but what they forgot to mention (and more importantly, weren't reminded of by Republicans) was that he obviously wasn't this evil Rich Uncle

Pennybags that he was made out to be because he gave up millions of dollars to walk away from his business to make a positive change in our country.

I feel like rather than fight back and go toe-to-toe with their enemy, the GOP goes soft and turns the other cheek. And it sucks to watch on the sidelines as a fan of the team.

It's the same thing, over and over and over again.

The Republicans get whooped on message, they get whooped on coalitions to minorities and young people, and they get whooped in elections. It's almost as if we follow the "good defense is the best offense," strategy rather than going on the offense. And sure, that could work once in a while, like when the Baltimore Ravens won the Superbowl over a decade ago with a crappy quarterback that was never heard from again, but at that point, they had a record-setting defense. Their defense was so tough that they would move the football back up the other side of the field. They were sacking the other teams quarterback and getting turnover after turnover. And if you don't know football, I just spoke a foreign language to you, but the bottom line is that if your defense can't basically be so aggressive that it turns into an offense and literally scares the other team, you're going to need to go on the offensive once in a while.

Maybe it's just time to stop being nice. The Democrats are almost always on the attack against the GOP. They don't miss a moment to mock something that they've done and if the actual politicos don't catch it, then the incredible writing staff at either *The Daily Show* or *The Colbert Report* and the alright writing staff at *Saturday Night Live* are there to pick up the pieces for them. Sure, they also make fun of the left once in a while, but for the most part, those shows are set up to make fun of the right...and there's nothing wrong with it, because we give them plenty to make fun of.

Take a look at the appeal our party has to the American people and ask yourself, "Where are the Republican All-Stars?"

It's easy to call out the stars of the Democratic Party: Barack Obama, Hillary Clinton, Bill Clinton, Joe Biden, Nancy Pelosi, and Martin O'Malley.

Now name stars of the Republican Party: John Boehner, John McCain, Ted Cruz, Marco Rubio, Sarah Palin, Eric Cantor, that Bobby Jindal, and Chris Christie.

Now take both those lists and narrow them down to the people who are only endorsed by the entire party; that means there isn't debate on their political ideologies.

When you look at the left, that list stays exactly the same minus the Governor of New Jersey who Republicans occasionally love: Barack Obama, Hillary Clinton, Bill Clinton, Joe Biden, Nancy Pelosi, and Martin O'Malley.

When you analyze the names on the right, they all disappear. I wouldn't even consider John McCain a star anymore; I just wanted to throw his name in there to make it seem like more of a balanced list.

Republicans can't even agree right now on who are their top stars and who aren't. There just isn't a "farm team" of politicians who are charismatic, experienced, and carrying the divided voters of this party. Even Mitt Romney in the last election was hotly debated *after* he was nominated.

The fact that people were voting because they didn't like Obama rather than the fact that they really supported the former Governor of Massachusetts should bother you as a Republican. You should ask what has happened to your team that it's come to that. Where are the stars? Where are the uniting forces?

We can't all keep clinging to Ronald Reagan because he's already past all his term limits. Yes, he had great ideas and was a great president, but we can't clone him and vote him back into office. The fact that he is the only candidate that it seems like all Republicans get behind is scary. Where's that modern charismatic thought leader who can take this country forward in the right direction?

Do you know what happens when you date a woman and don't stop talking about how great your ex-girlfriend was? You get dumped and you end up alone. Compare that to what you're doing to the modern Republican Party by clinging to how great Reagan was all the time.

It was like the GOP unanimously had a conversation with Mitt Romney wherein they said, "Hey Mitt, we really like you, but did you ever hear about our really great president Ronald Reagan?!?!"

Mitt could go on and on about his economic policies that could have turned this country around and it seemed like the GOP voters would keep on their Reagan rant, "He even had jelly beans on his desk, Mitt. Jelly beans! Are you going to put jelly beans in the White House, Mitt? Are you?"

The conversation from the Republican side should have gone more like, "Mitt Romney is the man! He's going to change this country and whoop Barack Obama at everything including basketball, which seems impossible, but Mitt is so good that he'll also dominate the president at a sport that he's definitely never played and has no viable skills in!"

And then there would be some sort of crazy rock song and fireworks that would play behind him. Instead, we had Mitt speak to a mildly warm crowd at the Republican National Convention who were all excited about Ronald Reagan and walk off stage to a live band cover of James Brown's classic, "Livin' In America."

Cue the fail horn.

At least pretend that you're unified behind a presidential candidate, right?

Now it just seems like Republican voters aren't thrilled with anything that's put up in front of them. If you really think about it, in the 2012 primary election season, we saw all the potential candidates the party really had to throw at us. That list included Newt Gingrich, Gary Johnson, Michelle Bachmann, Herman Cain, Rick Santorum, Mitt, and even Sarah Palin, who was just around to sell books. For the most part, each one of these people got what they were in it for, whether it be the actual nomination or a book, radio and television deal. These were the "stars" that the party had, and it didn't work…well it didn't work for the voters. Again, the candidates themselves did okay. In fact, if this book doesn't work, maybe I'll run for the Republican nomination in 2016 so that I can get a hell of a lot more popular to the point that I get at TV deal.

Did you *really* think that Herman Cain or any of the others were going to win the nomination? Be honest with yourself.

The real issue that I and many other Republicans had with the entire process was the feeling of "So this is all we've got?"

Had we all just supported Mitt from the beginning, we would've had a serious fighting chance to win the thing, but instead, we spent time spinning wheels on not-so-charismatic people with stupid taglines and books to sell. Have we learned our lesson yet?

Shouldn't we have pulled some of those candidates over to the side at the beginning and said "Hey…you can't be serious, can you? Drop out."

Even the Democrats, who started with a wide field in 2004, narrowed it down to Hillary and Obama quickly because they knew they were the viable candidates out of the pack. Here people were clinging on for seemingly nothing except airtime.

And when your party isn't excited about its candidate and doesn't fight back against attacks, you're just asking to be mocked and made fun of, basically made to look weak in front of the entire nation on a daily basis…or after every debate…which seemed to occur every other day.

So what is the right doing when the left is manipulating their tales and successfully working with the media? How are they reaching the people that need to be reached and planting an offensive to counteract the constant attacks?

Right now, it seems like they aren't doing anything. You see, I hate both Democrats and Republicans, because the Democrats are stomping all over the right and doing whatever they want because their strategies have worked, and on the other side, Republicans are falling into basic political traps, popularity contests, or just plain letting it happen.

If you're reading this and lean right, you're going to agree with me. If you're reading this and lean left, you're going to argue with it, but know if Republicans do start to change, your team is going to be in some serious trouble."

*That was written five years ago...*and what changed in that time? A gritty, mouthy, DGAF billionaire named Donald Trump stood up and became the loud hero supporting character I had said the GOP needed. Additionally, the Democrats put up the non-sexy, nasty, and barely charismatic Hillary Clinton to face him.

That was also a really long quote of mine from five years ago. You'll have to look back a few pages to see where it began, but those quotes are there at the beginning and end.

Not only did the Republicans find the solution that I was thinking they needed half a decade ago. Democrats ignored what had been historically working for them to move forward with a new path...an elderly, out-of-touch, politically elitist woman. Remember what worked with Obama? She wasn't anywhere near that.

CHAPTER 6:

★ ★ ★

CRAZY PEOPLE ON BOTH THE RIGHT AND THE LEFT?

I actually can't believe that we live in a society with such free flow of information and still come up with conspiracies about how our government is run and how it's going to end. For a while, it seemed as if it was *always* the Republicans or right-leaning people who believed in the crazy conspiracies…until the 2016 election of Donald Trump when the left couldn't believe they had lost. It was like suddenly after forty years, the left said to themselves, "What's this red scare that seems to be all the rage?"

Back to them in a bit, but let's start with Republicans.

Do you want to know why Republicans get a bad rap being called "conspiracy nuts" or "crazy" or whatever other iteration of crazy there is out there? Because there *are* crazy Republican conspiracy nuts out there, that's why!

Let's start with the most glaringly obvious pieces of garbage that was carried by our friends on the right: Birtherism.

As much as I wish it weren't, the theory is still out that that Obama is a Kenyan who happened to move to America and then somehow took on an evil plot to become president.

Shame on whichever Republicans are still clinging to that. You are the people who the media will focus on when they get the chance to ask you all sorts of ridiculous questions about your conspiracy beliefs and make other Republicans look crazy.

Come on, people. Pull it together. I want to break down this non-issue for you so that you can see just how ridiculous you look.

Let's jump right into this by looking at the fact that for it to have been real, *all fifty states* and their attorneys general ignored the fact that Barack Obama didn't have a birth certificate both times he ran for office and was elected. All of them.

That seems to be a bit much, don't you think? Each and every single attorney general in America forgot to check to see if a major candidate was an American citizen?

Let's give benefit of the doubt and say that all the Democrat run states were in on this grand scam that was run by their own party. That leaves roughly half the states in the Union who were run by very intelligent Republicans…including Texas, whose Governor in 2008 was starting to think about taking a stab at running the country as well. Don't you think that at least Texas would've put a stop to a non-citizen running for president? Come on.

So what you're essentially saying if you're a birther isn't just that Obama isn't an American; it's also that your Republican leadership in each and every one of those states who had a Republican attorney general are a bunch of lazy idiots who didn't think to run the essential required background check on a presidential candidate in order for them to be placed on a ballot.

You're saying that your Republican elected officials are stupid—and not just saying that Republican elected officials are stupid—you're also saying that the Republican National Committee is stupid and that the billions of dollars of campaigns and their staff between John McCain and Mitt Romney were also stupid… well that part might be believable at this point. But then, they wanted to win, so no.

When you're in a campaign, you look for absolutely everything that you can think of to eliminate your opponent without having to actually campaign. It's called working smarter, not harder. If you don't think that any of those thousands of people checked to see if then-Senator Obama or president-elect Obama was actually a natural born United States citizen, then you're completely out of your mind.

Oh, what else? There was that author bio that Barack Obama wrote about himself where he called himself a Kenyan and not an American. That *has* to prove it, right?

No, it doesn't. I'm willing to bet that his big book agent and the big book company that he was going to write for told him to spice up his bio. Being born in Hawaii doesn't really make you that exciting unless you went on to work with the crew of *5-0* or you're Dog the Bounty Hunter. Other than that, it sounds like you lived a life of luxury and makes you kind of bland. So why not spice it up with a little lie about your heritage? After all, no one's going to check it. It's not like you're running for president at that point in your life. Does that author bio make our president a liar at a young age? Yes. But does it make him anything other than that? No.

What about my author bio? Is it full of lies? Probably. You can check it if you want, but I am not running for president at this point in my life either, so no sweat off my back.

Writing books is just about entertaining people. Sure, you can inform them, but if your book isn't entertaining, it's not going to go well. Being born in Kenya as opposed to Hawaii is smart branding for an author. "Barack Obama came from a foreign land that was really poor and made it all the way to Harvard Law." That sounds incredibly entertaining. As opposed to "Barry Soetero grew up in the popular honeymoon destination of Hawaii, then moved around the United States with his family and ended up at Harvard Law." There's depth to the first one with the lie; the second is blah. See the difference? He lied then, which just shows he has a propensity of exaggeration and lying.

The final piece of evidence that shows that he was born a United States citizen is something much more convincing than anything else I've said to show that he wasn't lying. It's the fact that he ran against another someone who at the time he began running had a much more powerful last name than his own: Hillary Clinton.

If you don't think that the Clintons, with their overwhelming influence and power in politics didn't do all their research on Barack Obama to make sure that he was a citizen and to ensure that he was qualified in all ways to be president of the United States, then you should be locked away.

Without reviewing all the deals and political manipulations around the world that the Clintons have had their hands in, both good and bad, no one on either side of the aisle would believe that they would allow power to slip away from them that easily. Hillary and Obama had the Democratic Party divided in 2008 when they were running to be nominated for president, you can best believe that she had every detail about the man's life that you could ever want to know. And if he were born in Kenya, the Clintons would have exposed that and ended his political career right then and there. There would have never been a 2016 election against Donald Trump; we would all be living in whatever corrupt police state where Hillary was on our money and Mount Rushmore as well. It's really that simple.

Republicans, if you still believe that Barack Obama wasn't born in America, please feel free to go back into your underground lair and listen to more of Alex Jones and *InfoWars* on your crank-up radio. Oh, you didn't think I'd skip out on this guy, do you?

Alex Jones is one of the top sources of information for every single crazy Republican. I again say that because the left at least hides their crazies better than we do. And there's a reason that he feeds incredible information to the crazier amongst us. One word that describes lots of green paper and rhymes with "honey."

Let's do a little bit of background on this before we break into some of the more "fun" stories.

Do you know what preppers are?

There are old shows on *The Discovery Channel* about them, including *Doomsday Preppers*. These are shows about people who think the end of the world is coming. Not like end, end of the world where a religious icon comes back and burns everything up, but rather the end of the world as we know it. Preppers think that after a certain series of events happen, either caused naturally, politically, by economic collapse, or by one of our sworn enemies overseas, that they will be out there on their own.

The critical part of this is that they think they've got the jump on this before anyone else does. So they will store everything from water to freeze-dried corn, to canned corn, to bullets and guns, and even print-outs of information on how to do all sorts of medical things that you would *never* want to do on your own—literally everything you can think of. But the most important thing about preppers is that they spend tons of money to do this. Oh, and they all vote Republican.

Preppers think a lot about Barack Obama, including but not limited to him not being an American citizen, being Muslim, a lizard person, on the take from big banks—you name it, they believe it. And because they believe it, they are going to prepare for when he does something to ruin America.

There are a bunch of scenarios that I'll review in a bit that you'll laugh at that preppers believe in, but before we go there, let's look at Alex Jones.

Jones knows his audience and he knows what buttons to push to get them going. If you ever hear about fluoride in your water poisoning you, that came from him. Also, anything that happens with the TSA that seems negative has come from him as well.

He has at multiple points implied, if not stated, that there are higher powers that are training us to be led to our deaths and that the TSA is one of the major ways they're doing it. He's done TV specials where he shows where potential mass graves are around the country for when the government or whoever starts organ harvesting and decapitating us (yes, people believe that's going to happen). And one of my personal favorites: he has shown us "relocation facilities" where we will all be taken after a supposed fake national threat will occur and the government will start rounding up people to essentially put them in permanent custody.

Had enough yet? Did I mention that people who believe this, the preppers, are all Republican voters? See where people might start generalize that Republicans are crazy?

So even though there are explanations for a lot of things, like that the TSA are there to make sure that bombs don't get on planes or that fluoride is added to water in trace amounts to kill off potential bacteria that could kill you in the water, certain people are led down a path to believe that these poor saps at the airport making under twenty dollars an hour actually care enough to try to control us in order to take over the world, or that fluoride is put in the water to make sure stupid people die. Oh yes, the stupid people will die.

According to some higher power and their plot called eugenics, the government is working to kill off genetically stupid people, and rather than just go around giving out IQ tests and shooting people, they're slowly doing it by putting mouthwash ingredients in our water.

Maybe you logical people would understand it more if you were wearing a tinfoil hat. Take a break right now, go into your kitchen, and make a nice one for yourself. Add some horns or something to it to make it fancy and also so the aliens can send you messages about how to survive the coming whatever the hell is coming. The important thing that people like Alex Jones and *InfoWars* want you to know is that you're right and something *is definitely* coming.

In addition to ridiculous stockpiles of food, preppers also have get out of dodge or "go bags," so they can be ready for anything at any time. You never know when the economic collapse could happen and people all turn into zombies, so when that happens, you're going to need a bag with a crank-up radio, a flashlight, a couple of bottles of water and some army issued food rations (that taste terrible and are used by the same people who may or may not be taking your freedom depending on the scenario). It's actually not a bad idea to have one in case of a natural disaster. I certainly never saw the earthquake that hit DC a few years ago coming when I lived there. Had it been a lot worse, something like that might have helped had I had it handy. Unfortunately for the prepper, that little bit of a bag just isn't going to cut it.

You're also going to need a bunch of other junk to survive the coming apocalypse. Knives, training, bow and arrow, and you should also read the *Hunger Games* series because that's essentially what every single one of these crazy prepper scenarios ends up looking like.

The best part about it all? You can get all the supplies you need through Alex Jones' and his friends'/business partners' websites. How convenient!

While they're telling you that the world is coming to an end that all currency except gold and silver will no longer be accepted soon, they'll take most major credit cards, cash, and checks for their services.

Oh and did I mention his followers vote Republican, which allows Republicans to be overgeneralized and called crazy?

The best way for you to really understand how preppers operate and think is to watch every single *James Bond* movie and imagine believing in that plot, minus the cool British super agent character that saves the world and gets us out of it.

I'm not kidding either.

Prepper conspiracies include:

1. Goldeneye's EMP Attacks: Don't know what an electromagnetic pulse is? What rock have you been living under? Even Newt Gingrich mentioned them once. In Goldeneye, the Russians have an evil weapon that when it hits America or wherever the target is, will shut down all electronics. Just fry them all at once. So no more TV, no more computers, planes drop out of the air, and forget heating up last night's leftovers in a microwave. When an EMP attack hits, we are going to be without electricity forever. This conspiracy is also ripped off for the critical plot of the TV show Revolution. Yawn. It's been done, people. It's been done.

2. In On Her Majesty's Secret Service, the villain makes plants and animals sterile so they can no longer produce food for us to eat. That would give him the ability to take over the world by controlling the food supply. A lot of prepper websites tell us that we need to get heirloom seeds and that seeds will be more valuable than gold if we lose power or there is a government takeover just because of that. Buy now or else you're going to be in trouble.

3. In A View to a Kill, there is a plot to take out Silicon Valley and thus control where all the technology in the world is created. Also, EMP attacks are mentioned here.

4. In Tomorrow Never Dies, there is an evil plot to take over all the media in the world. Don't think for a moment that this is the theory that liberals control the media, because well, for the most part, news organizations lean right. I'm talking full-scale world takeover of all the media outlets by a group who wants to control all the rights of humankind!

5. In Skyfall, the villain is a hacker who can control anything, including the power grids, trains—anything you can think of—and shut them down whenever he wants. If there's one thing that our grandparents fear, it's the internet. Let's face it, most of us either have the type of grandparents who are all up in our space on Facebook or they fear the internet because it's a land of filth and pornography. The fact that the internet is actually a land of filth and pornography aside, those grandparents who believe that also believe that the world can be taken over using those same evil interwebs. This is actually the closest to being a legitimate threat of all of these. And even then, that threat is far from coming to fruition.

And finally, my most favorite:

1. In *Quantum of Solace*, the villain wants to control the water supply of African nations to control all the power there. Yes, there is a theory that there will be a war for the water supply in this country…and who do preppers think is going to start World War III for water? China! Their *actual* theory is that the Chinese will cross over the Pacific Ocean to fight us for our clean water supply. Let me repeat that. There is a group of people who believe

that the Chinese will cross over the largest ocean on the planet to start World War III for water!

As funny as it seems, there is a growing amount of people out there who believe that the world as we know it is coming to an end. Sadly, they are crazy, and that craziness all gets generalized to Republicans. These are also the fun types of people whom the media drools to get on television at Trump rallies.

You may not remember this, but years ago at the end of the government shutdown under Obama, the House of Representatives stenographer yelled, "He will not be mocked! The greatest deception here is this is not one nation under God. It never was. The Constitution would not have been written by freemasons. They go against God. You cannot serve two masters."

Yeah, I'm willing to bet she was a prepper.

Oh, and how exactly am I an expert in preppers? Did I happen to mention that on the side, I'm a copywriter who wrote copy for prepper websites for years?

Back to Alex Jones and *InfoWars,* who were competitors of the companies I wrote for…and regularly beat by the way. The sad thing is that every so often, he and his staff break some really good news…it is however mixed in with so much other nonsensical and overblown stuff that it costs him the credibility that he might deserve in that one instance. Oh and one more thing on him: in his custody case for his children, his lawyer said his entire gimmick is just an act.

So. There's. That.

Don't get too excited thinking that the right has all the crazies either. Democrats have a significant pile of nutcases, but the press and the party don't shine spotlights on them. For the most part, when we hear from them, we're told immediately that they are a joke so that you giggle at something they did rather than get offended by it. Who are they? Let's cover the traditional crazies first, then we'll get to the Trump-era folks.

The first set of nuts on the left are your run-of-the-mill hippies, or in more modern times, the type of person who would fall into the hipster demographic.

Who can forget the life and times of the 1960s? Hippies certainly can't. You'll find hippies still out there, protesting for animals or chaining themselves to trees to help save Mother Earth.

The modern hippie has three major goals and I will present them here in hippie speak:

1. We gotta stop corporate greed maaaaaan.

2. We gotta protect the earth and the animals from people who are all destroying it and stuuuuuuffffffff.

3. We gotta legalize weed maaaaan. It makes no sense that it's illegal.

That's it. That's your modern hippie. And how they go about it is the best.

If you've ever seen *Portlandia* or visited Portland or my previous hometown of Austin, you'd completely understand their lifestyle. When I moved to Austin, I thought for some reason that I would be moving to Texas, but that was a mistake. In fact, Austin is one of the bluest of the blue cities in the nation. It isn't "Texas" other than by location. I also moved to the east side of town, which is the bluest of the bluest of blue or as some of you might say, one of the more eclectic parts of the country.

I was accepted into and fit into hippie/hipster culture well because of how I dress and act most of the time. Because I lived on the east side of the city but worked downtown, I'd frequently ride my bike everywhere; I like to eat healthy, so often I eat vegetarian; and I basically only wear thrift shop clothing because nothing beats wearing a comfortable t-shirt with a crazy-looking sport coat over it on stage or in a meeting. I look, act, and eat like a hipster, but I'm far from one.

Being that I lean right, but dress left, I've found myself dating their women, and generally being accepted by the craziest of the left-wingers in town. That privilege allows me to know exactly how they tick.

The bottom line is that they are the masters of taking what could be a good idea and riding it right off the rails into insanity!

I think we can all agree that we should work to lower pollution. Pollution is bad.

We don't want to be breathing smog in every day because breathing smog in sucks.

If you've ever been to southeast Asia, you actually have to adjust to the level of smog in the air. It's tough to breathe for a bit once you get there because of all the motorbikes and industry in major cities around you. We have no conditions even remotely similar to that in America, so trust me, clean air is the best. And if I can do my part once in a while by riding my bike or cutting back on a little bit of a product that causes a lot of pollution, I will, but that's really the extent of it from me. Hippies don't stop with a little bit of helping out. They have to take things so far that it becomes laughable.

When I first moved to Austin, I looked on Craigslist for an apartment like any cheap person would do. I really liked the picture of a house that I saw on there because it was so incredibly cheap and was about to call the number for it, but I couldn't get over a certain nuance in the description.

The ad said something along the lines of, "Must not mind only flushing toilets once a day or less." My curiosity got the best of me and I called the people. Apparently, they would only flush the toilets a couple of times a week to pitch in for the environment and save water. That's right; you would all poop and pee in a shared toilet in the house and I guess one lucky person would get so sick of the odor at some point you would finally cave and destroy the world a little bit by flushing.

If it was up to them, they would probably just eliminate toilets and that use of water altogether in order to save the environment. That would never do anything terrible to the world. I mean it's not like the spread of black plague amongst other plagues was caused by a lack of proper sewage disposal in the olden days or anything.

These extreme people are the same ones who make their own soaps and toothpastes and don't use deodorant because of the chemicals in them. After all, it's better to stink to holy hell rather than keep your body clean, right?

The best hippies don't shave either, which means that that odor sticks around in their hair for even longer. I hope you're eating while you're reading this book.

Just keep in mind that these people stink up voting booths while they're voting for the Democrats.

Another way that they want to save the environment? Making it illegal for businesses to use plastic straws. Recently, the city of Santa Barbara, California not only made it illegal to distribute straws, but attached a six-month jail sentence and one thousand dollar fine if you're found guilty of it. That's not even remotely logical and takes a good idea, cutting back on pollution, to a laughable extreme.

Here's another good idea gone wrong. Hippies/hipsters don't want to eat food that's been chemically treated. This actually makes a lot of sense. I don't want to eat apples that are coated in wax and I certainly don't want to eat meats that have been given steroids to grow. So here they are again, starting with a logical, winnable base level. It starts to spin out of control quickly when everything has to be free range and they actually talk to the animals.

I was recently in Denver where they have an "all-natural farm-to-table" restaurant. The food there wasn't that bad, but the server couldn't stop talking about the mission of the place and how incredible the chef there was. In her words, the animals that were "sacrificed" for our meals didn't go un-loved. They lived on a farm where they were permitted to do whatever they wanted to do. No one restricted them with cages. Then, a few days before each "sacrifice," the chef would go and live on the farm with the animals. He would name each animal and stay with them, feeding them and letting them get to love and nurture their children before he would humanely "sacrifice" them to make the food that we were about to eat.

I was reassured that he loved each and every animal and treated them all with dignity and respect before he knocked them off by slicing their throats or whatever to make bacon or hamburgers or chicken fingers. After a no less than six-minute talk about how much love the chef has for the animals, the server finally left us alone to place our orders. I stopped, stared at my friend, because I was already trying not to laugh and said, "I'm not ordering meat here."

"Why? It sounds like good stuff," said my friend.

"You didn't get the vibe that I did from that rant about the chef and the animals?" I asked my friend and stared blankly until I got the response we were both thinking.

Finally, after forty-five seconds and a strained look of deep thought on her face, she said, "Okay, you win. He definitely has sex with the animals."

Yes. That's how bad the love of those animals was. He was so passionate that he would feed them, name them, love them, talk to their children, and live in the open fields with them, that the only conclusion we had was that he *really loved* those animals.

We both ordered vegetable dishes and they were just okay... nothing too special, but you're not here for a Yelp review so I'll keep the story moving. After all of that love, maybe we should've gone with the meat? Nah, gross.

Just like preppers on the Republican side, there are people waiting to sucker in hippies/hipsters on the Democrat side and grab their money. This place was one of them. The vegetable plates we had were incredibly overpriced, and the sales pitch on some of the upsold items were equally as ridiculous.

"Do you want to try some of our incredible vegan ketchup? It's only three dollars and fifty cents for a six ounce bottle"—The Waitress

"Am I missing something? Isn't all ketchup vegan?"—Me

"No, not all ketchup is vegan that I know of. But you can be assured with ours that it is."—The Waitress

"All ketchup is vegan. It's made from tomatoes, vinegar and sugar. None of those items come from an animal."—Me

The waitress went silent. You can buy a half gallon of ketchup for three dollars and fifty cents, let alone six ounces of it. And it's all vegan. Other vegan condiments include soy sauce, mustard, relish, BBQ sauce, and anything else that's made entirely out of vegetables. Basically, everything excluding mayonnaise is vegan. But branding and prices would tell you differently.

The biggest hit to hippies and hipsters comes from certified organic produce. If you ever get to go to a supermarket and see the difference in pricing, you'll see that the organic stuff is about a dollar more a pound. Let's avoid getting into the rules and regulations and benefits to farmers that the government does or doesn't give them and let's focus on organic and certified organic produce, because that's all that hippies will eat, after all; that's what comes directly from Mother Earth and is unfettered by human chemicals, right?

Not quite. It's got chemicals in it, but, they're just in a safer category than the other stuff that might be in it. Essentially, and I know a lot of you will argue this with me…organic and not organic really doesn't make a difference unless you're eating your body weight-plus a day in the regular, non-organic stuff. If you ever do that, you're gonna die of some sort of terrible cancer…but you'll never do that.

Organic green apples or regular green apples? Well, a hippie or a health nut would obviously go organic, but that doesn't make a difference other than putting an extra word on the package and charging an extra dollar a pound. Add up all those dollars and by simply labeling a package a little bit differently and doing practically *nothing else*, farmers are cleaning up on hippies and well, most other unknowing people as well. But in this case, let's keep focusing on those hippies.

Hippies are a great crazy asset to the left and not just as voters. Since most media outlets spin their news to the left, they won't waste time speaking to "Dove Harmony Sunshine" and her friend "Harvest Moon Happiness" at the local pro-choice rally. It wouldn't make sense to waste the airtime making their team look bad. Knowing that, Democrats pay them a bit, bus them in, and fill fields full of stinky hippies to make protests look bigger. They sometimes even get them to bring their drums from their drum circles to make more of an impact.

My favorite experience with hippies is what I tell on stage as my defining Austin moment.

I love a certain vegan restaurant in Austin that shall remain nameless for the sake of this story.

One Friday night, I wanted to take a woman out on a date to a crazy fun place with good food. Something so uniquely Austin that she would get a kick out of it. And so I chose this vegan restaurant. See, when someone says that something is "uniquely Austin," it means confidently bizarre…or simply weird. After all, that's why someone coined the phrase, "Keep Austin Weird"—people here just kind of do their own thing. They smoke a ton of weed, don't accomplish too much, dress like I do (so I can't knock it), and live their best free-spirited lives, maaaaan.

This restaurant is no different. When you walk inside, you're almost immediately hit with a color of paint that can only be described as a retina-burning aqua. It's as if the designer of the place walked into Home Depot and asked where the clearance paint no one wanted was located. Upon seeing that pile of refuse, they returned to the customer service counter and asked for the cheaper stuff. The representative took them to a pile of paint cans in the back alley and said, "Hey listen, this paint is free, but I've gotta warn you, if you stare at it for too long, your eyes will actually start to catch fire." The designer was thrilled and painted every last corner of the restaurant with that paint.

Not only are you greeted with the feeling of your retinas burning, but you hear music that you vaguely recognize from your childhood. Not a good part of your childhood either, but that night that you scarred by watching a 1970s rape-horror movie that should have never been produced but airs nonstop at like 3 AM on an off network that you're too tired to change the channel on. They have all the complete soundtracks to that music on a jukebox playing constantly in the corner.

To top it all off, there are also typically decorations around the place that can only be described as "I don't know what the hell they are."

That night I was informed by the server that there was live music on the patio. Now I hadn't recalled hearing live music on the porch when we were walking up, but I thought to myself "Hey, this has got to be something spectacular out here; sign me up." So we switched our seats to seats on the patio.

Not much of a surprise, we were the only people out there and in the corner of the patio wasn't a band or a man playing a normal solo instrument like an accordion at a French restaurant or an acoustic guitar. No, this guy had a trombone. The best part? He was disappointed that someone had shown up to hear him play.

He began playing whatever song you play on a trombone. I played in jazz band in high school and never heard anything other than a crappy trombone solo, so that's basically what it sounded like, but worse. He played seemingly against his will for the longest five minutes of our lives what sounded like a cover of one of the rape-horror classics from inside. Then he stopped and yelled over to us, "Hey, you got any requests?"

We both looked at each other and couldn't think of anything creative because let's face it, *no one knows any trombone songs,* so I responded "no."

His immediate response was, "Wellp, then I'm getting the fuck outta here. Peace man." And he packed up his stuff, collected what looked to be pay from the owner, and went along his merry way.

That, my friends, is the epitome of the modern hippie. Someone who like a lost member of a marching band plays a trombone solo for five minutes at a vegan restaurant with ambiance that's designed to not only make you go blind, but to give you horrible nightmares, and who upon not having direction from you, decides his job is over, but that he's still deserving of pay for that extraordinarily terrible feat.

Oh, and on top of all of this, I'm sure he votes Democrat.

The final hippie that I wanted to talk about is the legalize weed guy. Everyone in a major city knows this guy. All he talks about is how he wants to legalize weed and how the Republicans are stodgy old men who want to keep him down, maaaaaaaan.

This guy is really a crazy one-trick pony. The problem with him is that he's a self-defeating one trick pony. See, he's stoned all the time…that goes without saying. He's the one with the hemp seeds that he eats in the morning and hemp shirts, hemp stickers, hemp computers, hemp cars and whatever else you can make from hemp. If you've got a hemp pile of poop, he'll make a pamphlet about it to tell other people about how great hemp poop is. Why? Because he is the biggest activist for legalizing weed, and he is also the biggest user of weed in the neighborhood. Marijuana *is* his life.

In fact, if you ask him what he does, typically this guy will tell you about a good job he almost had or almost had at one time but that corporate America hated on him and took away that job because of drug testing. So what's he doing now? If he's not a roadie for a band, he's probably just selling weed for a living.

I mean really if you think about it, when you work at a gas station, you get all the free gas that you want, right? Don't ruin that example for me; it seems logical…So for the guy who is all about weed, what better job than selling it?

The problem is that if you're selling weed and weed gets legalized, you lose your job. Stores aren't going to hire a pothead drug dealer because he was selling off parts of his stash to his buddies for extra cash. Sadly, if he were to win his uphill battle against the evil suppression of drugs, he would be unemployed. But, if you think about it, if the right liberals were in office to legalize weed, he would probably be in a great position to file as a former drug dealer for unemployment benefits. That way he can smoke weed that's legal all day long on our dollar. All in all, this clueless guy gets to live the good life. Also, like some of the preppers, he might be stuck in his house on Election Day, but unlike them, he's not trying to hide from "Big Brother"; he's just too high to remember that it's Election Day. If for some reason he's sober enough, though, he's voting Democrat.

For the most part, that summarized all the crazy that there was on the left, up until the results of the 2016 presidential election came in.

Immediately after that, people lost their minds. Everything was offensive to them (except when they themselves said it) and there was no way that Donald Trump had just been elected president of the United States...no way!

From the woman (?) who instantly became a meme screaming "No!" at inauguration to the celebrities who screamed about vaginal blood running down their legs, a new level of insane happened. College students were suddenly triggered by not using the right pronouns to describe them and then there was that whole Russian collusion tinfoil hat thing.

Remember, when this all started, the narrative was that the Russian government had directly colluded with Donald Trump's campaign to aid in his election. That started to slip a bit then it turned into a Russian lawyer with connections to the Russian government had one meeting with the Trump campaign. Then that didn't really stick so it digressed more to Russians bought ads on Facebook and ran a few accounts on Twitter. Which is now only interference.... Then it was Russians hacked Hillary Clinton's illegal email server...where we forgot that she was the first person who committed the crime in order to pretend that only the Russians did bad...and this is a run-on sentence is designed to show you that we have now stretched far beyond collusion between Donald Trump's campaign and the Russian government to scream about the red scare every single time that Russia or Trump's election is brought up.

Forget the fact that Trump administration has done more to hurt Russia than the past 3 administrations and also forget the fact that he railed on Germany at NATO for cutting a multi-billion dollar deal to get energy from them...Trump, to many of tinfoil-hat wearing people on the left, is a "Putin Puppet" and someone who would not have won had it not been for Russia.

That's right, Russia caused 62,984,825 people to vote for Trump. I knew it...and this all stems from the craziest on the left's inability to accept that they just didn't win the last presidential election.

★ ★ ★

CHAPTER 7

IF YOU'RE GOING TO BE A "RELIGIOUS NUT," AT LEAST DO IT RIGHT

My favorite criticism of Republicans is that they're crazy about Jesus, to the point that it clouds all the rest of their logical judgment in their lives. I've been told over and over again by my progressive friends that religious Republicans are hateful, spiteful, evil people who do nothing more than spread fear and hatred about things like homosexuality and abortion. I think I left some "hates" out of that, but the question is, are they like that?

The answer isn't no, but it also isn't quite yes either.

Let's start with the better question: why are gay marriage and women's issues front and center when our government is disorganized to the point of shutdown and we seem to be at the brink of war with God knows who?

The easy answer to that question is because it started as a distraction from the fact that Obama is failing on fiscal policy, then reached into one of the few things that Democrats have left to fight with Republicans on.

You might recall during the 2008 presidential election, we magically heard from a list of nobody's like Sandra Fluke (pronounced like the F-word with an L than the actual word fluke which would better explain her fifteen minutes of fame). These types of women came out of the woodwork in order to declare that there was a Republican "War on Women." Can't fault them for coming up with a catchy tagline, right? How else would you distract from the real issues of the economy and our country's infrastructure basically falling apart at the time? And I'll be damned if it wasn't catchy enough to stick around even through today.

Sandra Fluke wasn't all the Democrat's concoction either. We can thank Rush Limbaugh for her. When he made the grave mistake of calling her a slut on air, the DNC pounced and elevated the unknown-at-the-time-and-thankfully-unknown-again thirty-year old law student to a heroic level. She was the example of how mean Republicans were. You know, they hate women and gays and anyone who isn't a white male right? That's what this issue is always nuclear exploded into, even when it's just one comment about one woman.

Apparently, the people in charge of the Republican strategy and *The Rush Limbaugh Show* at the time never paid attention to the characters in law school or else they would've known better. Fluke was the perfect example of a liberal woman who finds everything offensive and is just lying in wait to complain about everything and anything. She was the type of character who would make the case for spelling women with a "y" because she doesn't want "men" in her word if she had the chance. The people in charge of the strategy at the time did *nothing* to counteract her, but instead elevated her to a pedestal by continuing to insult her. Luckily over time she went away, but there have been dozens of nationalized victims since because the strategy works. That aside...

We had to be force-fed the war on women throughout the entire campaign because no one stood up to call a duck a duck. This was a stunt to get the attention away from actual issues like America's terrible economy and debt for which Obama was clearly responsible...and it worked.

That same cycle, Hilary Rosen, a now forgotten democratic strategist and pundit on CNN knocked Ann Romney (long groan: Mitt's wife) for "never working a day in her life." Sure, the GOP fired back a bit and Rosen apologized for her comments, but the Republican Party then forgave and forgot (like a good Christian and a *bad campaign* would). You see, Democrats don't forget when something happens, and they continued to beat the Sandra Fluke story to death, literally stretching her fifteen minutes to around seventeen and a half. She even got to speak at the Democratic National Convention, which proves to me that the only qualification for speaking at the DNC is being called a slut by a prominent Republican pundit. By those standards, I should have been a keynote there a few cycles in a row.

Not to sound like I'm cheaping out on social issues, but just about any social issue that Republicans get beat up on for not supporting is a million times worse in a "religion of peace" country. Oh, did you forget that Christians are evil, but the Islamic faith, the "religion of peace" is a warm and fuzzy land of hugs and happiness that we should support because progressives tell us to do so?

I mean, it's not like there's a list of the top most dangerous countries for women and those countries are dominated by the hug of happiness that is Islam, right? Wait, there is? And a majority of those top-ranked countries are dominated by the Islamic faith? Women can't vote, there are honor killings, and they're treated like possessions in most of those countries on top of all the raping and other disgusting acts carried out on women, but Republicans in America are the terrible ones, right?

One of the greatest hypocrisies that exists in today's world is the belief that you can be a progressive woman and be a Muslim. Women in the fundamentalist Muslim sects are treated like property. They are forced to cover themselves from head to toe and even most of their faces for religious purposes and to honor their husbands, who are the only people allowed to see them. Why? Because they are the possession of their husband and their faith in a patriarchal society. I think women are beautiful, and when I date a beautiful woman, I want the world to see her.

I couldn't imagine asking my girlfriend to cover herself up so that no other man could see her body but me. Instructing a woman how to dress is the beginning of the downward spiral of domestic abuse that happens in America more often than you would think, but I guess if it's gone on for your entire life or hundreds of years in another country, then it's okay.

Women should be able to wear what they want when they want to wear it. Critics here will say, "Well, then women should be allowed to wear a hijab and outfit that covers them from head to toe. Sure, they can if they want, but they aren't allowed to call themselves free or progressive. No progressive woman would subject herself to being treated like a piece of property that can only be seen by certain men. Notice I didn't even cover how many women could vote or not, because it overlaps with most of the cultures where they have to cover themselves for God or whatever. Just know you can't say you're all for women's rights when you yourself are a victim of one of the oldest wars on women in the history of the world. Sure, they say the GOP is the one who has waged this war, but we forget that in the countries of this "religion of peace," women actually get stoned or honor killed for attempting to be free and think on their own.

Oh, did you also know that Republicans hate gays? Forget the fact that I know quite a few gay Republicans and some that should probably just give up and come out of the closet…. We were told by the media machine and the left that anyone who didn't support gay marriage was homophobic and hated gays. Not that their religion didn't approve of homosexuality, no. They *hated* gays.

And of course the people whom the finger was pointed at were conservative Christians. You know, those "horrible people" who hate others rather than believe in the word of God that has been handed to them. You can't fault someone for being a conservative Christian, can you? Oh, that's right, the left can. That's why they wanted God taken out of their platform at the DNC. Who can forget when they booed God…. *Booed God.*

Now listen, I believe in God, but even if I didn't. I'm not going to be stupid enough to boo a higher power. What if I were wrong? I could get struck by lightning or disease or anything else that different Gods pull out to punish others…yikes.

We also forget about that "peaceful religion" of Islam and how they treat gay people. Muslims in the Middle East are typically extremely violent against gay people. Bahrain, Kuwait, Qatar, Oman, Saudi Arabia, and the United Arab Emirates have laws against being gay. Not gay marriage—just being gay. You get locked in jail or tortured for being gay. Not only is it illegal to be gay, they are going that extra step to medically test people to see if they're gay. How do you medically test someone to see if they're gay? Poke and prod at them for hours and then play some show tunes to see if they sing along?

But Republicans are the hateful ones. Christians who only disapprove of gays getting married are the hateful ones.

Side note: seventy-eight countries around the world have made being gay illegal, but being lesbian is only illegal in forty-nine. I guess it's cool if it's hot chicks, but apparently it's *never* cool if it's dudes.

Back to Obama. Remember how he loved women and supported gay marriage? That's a completely organic, truthful point of view right? He would never have made that up for political gain, would he?

The first person to have mentioned that the Obama administration supported gay marriage was Vice President Joe Biden. Good for old Joe! Getting out there on his own before the president and making a statement, right? Wrong!

The very next week, the president declared that he was in support of gay marriage as well, but then a very interesting story leaked out of the White House...Joe was *reprimanded* for coming out (not as gay, but in support of gay marriage) out of turn and not on schedule with the Obama campaign's plan. Joe actually had to apologize to the boss for letting his support of gay marriage leak out of turn. But of course the president supports gay marriage and wants everyone to be equal on his own without political motives!

If I were gay and had my hopes up when Biden supported me, then I would feel completely used and let down by the follow-up apology and game playing showing that it was a mistimed stunt to get my vote. I mean, Republicans are the ones who hate gays and game the system to get votes! But wait, there's more.

Remember when Obama lifted the "Don't Ask, Don't Tell" policy in the military? He got some credit for that, but what you didn't see was when he closed down Lafayette Park, the one adjacent to the White House where there were gay soldiers who chained themselves to the White House fence to protest not only Don't Ask Don't Tell, but also gay marriage. This made our president look bad, so he ordered the park shut down so that media couldn't cover it…wait I'm sorry, according to Ben Smith at Politico at the time,

"UPDATE: **US Park Police spokesman David Schlosser tells POLITICO** his service erred in pushing the reporters back, and stressed that the White House played no role in the move.

'That was strictly the US Parks Police that screwed up—that has nothing to do with the Secret Service of the White House or the Administration,' said Sergeant Schlosser. 'We had some young officers who, when they were told to move the people back—which we typically do when we're going to make arrests—they moved the people back a lot further than we typically do. That was a rookie, amateur error and they screwed up on that.'

So see? It wasn't Barry and the campaign; it was a rookie cop who just wasn't good at his job who did that. Because they have rookie cops guarding the park around the White House, right? Come on.

Do you feel the wind coming off of that spin?

But Obama loved gays and gay marriage and wants equal rights, right? I mean it's not like he would go on a prominent network like MTV and completely bail on gay marriage two weeks before the election when it looked like he had it on lock…oh wait, according the man himself,

"It would be up to future generations of Americans to implement meaningful reform," when it comes to gay marriage.

Sorry I called MTV a prominent network, but as far as young people go, they have a snapchat story so it kind of is still relevant…I digress. He literally went on the young people's network and spit in their progressively blind supportive faces by backing off of his support of gay marriage. "Oh yeah, I'm all for it, but I'm not going to do anything about it." If that was any Republican on an issue, it would've been everywhere, but alas, it wasn't. It was the media king himself, Barack Obama.

When the Supreme Court finally ruled in support of gay marriage, Obama lit of the White House in rainbow colors and the streets were filled with celebrating people…as if he had anything to do with it and took a hard stand for it. He literally just took the credit and celebrated the victory when he had completely walked away from the issue.

So let's review, shall we?

Republicans are the hateful ones who don't support gays or women, but the left, who tells us that they *love* gays and women, support Muslim "peaceful cultures," which outlaw and torture gays and suppress women's rights. Then that same left are the ones who pigeonhole and villainize Republican women and flip-flop on gay marriage to get votes.

Seems like a simple conclusion here, right? We aren't done yet.

There are some of you Republicans and Christians out there that are hateful, and your disgusting statements and actions make the rest of the team look terrible.

I think it's critical that you read and believe all that's in that book that you reference all the time, so let's review a couple of points here.

Yes, the Bible says that being gay is wrong, but there's also the whole rest of the Bible where Jesus tells us how to behave, and it certainly doesn't involve being disgusted by others' actions and telling them they're going to burn in hell.

Let's get into some hot Bible action, shall we?

Read along:

Mark 2:13-17

13 Once again Jesus went out beside the lake. A large crowd came to him, and he began to teach them. 14 As he walked along, he saw Levi son of Alphaeus sitting at the tax collector's booth. "Follow me," Jesus told him, and Levi got up and followed him.

[15] While Jesus was having dinner at Levi's house, many tax collectors and sinners were eating with him and his disciples, for there were many who followed him. [16] When the teachers of the law who were Pharisees saw him eating with the sinners and tax collectors, they asked his disciples: "Why does he eat with tax collectors and sinners?"

[17] On hearing this, Jesus said to them, "It is not the healthy who need a doctor, but the sick. I have not come to call the righteous, but sinners."

Oh snap! What did Jesus do there? He ate with sinners. He didn't go to a huge protest and make signs to tell people they were going to burn in hell if they were wrong. Nope, instead he went and hung out with those people at whom the other religious people turned up their noses. Crazy idea, right? Instead of going and congregating with other like-minded people to talk about how great things were for him, he went and hung out with the people that didn't agree with him and was friendly.

Wow, if we acted like Jesus, we would have a whole lot more friends, wouldn't we? We'd be out there loving everyone, even those who are gay or might have had abortions or even those evil Democrats. See? Jesus had it right where a lot of you had it wrong. You aren't going to change the world if you aren't going to go and congregate with people who aren't like you. In this case, a lot of you Republicans who don't take the time to ask "WWJD?" are making the rest of us look terrible. You know who the media and the left are going to highlight, right? The "crazies." And the more that you put yourself out there as a loud voice against gay marriage holding a sign that says something like "It's not Adam and Steve," rather than going and making friends with those who you disagree with, the more the GOP is going to lose.

Here's another fun one for you Christians out there. There was an adulterous woman in the Bible who was going to be stoned, "religion of peace" style, but Jesus stopped the stoning in John 8:7 by saying,

> *"Let any one of you who is without sin be the first to throw a stone at her."*

I'm not finished yet—wait for this one—Romans 3:23 where it says,

> *"...for all have sinned and fall short of the glory of God..."*

See where I'm going with this. Essentially, any sin will keep you out of heaven, so as many theologians have said, sins are all equal. But it's certainly much easier to cast stones and point fingers at other people who sin. If you consider homosexuality a sin, and it is according to the Bible, who are you to point fingers and tell gay people that they are bad people? Don't you break laws when you speed? Don't you tell little fibs and gossip behind people's backs? Aren't you yourself probably gay and hiding it if you're really vocal about gay marriage being bad? (I had to go there; you had to see it coming.) I guarantee that each and every one of you who head to rallies to protest gay marriage or abortion and talk about how terrible those people are is just as guilty of sins of your own. But in this instance, you're casting stones when Jesus told you not to.

Not only that, you're making Republicans look terrible. *Terrible*. Instead of loving everyone, you're acting ignorantly. Now I'm not saying you can't change laws and congregate to discuss and protest that; don't get me wrong. I'm just saying to watch your rhetoric and how you do it, because you make your entire team look bad when you act like the ignorant fool that Jesus instructs you not to be.

There was another Bible verse I wanted to pull out as well. It's the one that's quoted the most but also ignored the most:

Matthew 22: 39

"... 'Love your neighbor as yourself.'"

Now I know that a lot of you have no problems loving yourself. I love myself more than most people love themselves, so I'm guilty of not following this, because I don't love anyone as much as I love me...But let's really take a look at that verse. You Christians who are out there not loving others and accepting people with their faults and sins are breaking what Jesus considered the second most important commandment. That's right: Christians, Republicans, conservatives, human beings...if you aren't loving others as much as you love you or as much as your God loves you, then you have no right to beat a Bible and the laws of God in their face.

Okay...I'll step down from the pulpit now. Don't get me wrong after all of that preaching; I think a lot of people are idiots and I will tell them that, but I also expect to be told that I'm an idiot and wrong as well, because more than occasionally, I am. It's my attempt at trying to be as equal in the love of others as myself.

Think about it though; Democrats, even if just selfishly for votes alone, are out there with open arms giving out hugs to everyone, the way that Jesus instructed us all to act...of course without doing it for the votes. That's why conservative Republicans get a bad rap. You're too busy being quoted saying how disgusted you are with gays and women who have abortions instead of being out there on the front line telling people that you love them.

Who would you vote for if you were a gay person or someone who had an abortion or a friend or family member of those people? The Republican who tells you you're wrong, or the Democrat who spins things to sound happy but doesn't cast stones at you for your sins? It's a no-brainer and it's one of the reasons that Democrats have the ability to make Republicans look so bad using very few facts and simple sound clips in the media.

I'm not saying to break from your faith or support something that you don't believe in, but what I am saying here is that if you want to be successful as a conservative, you need to be very cautious what you say on and off camera and what's on your signs. Why? Because the worst is what's going to be plastered everywhere and used against you forever. And sure, it's your First Amendment right to say whatever you want, but it's also your right to keep losing elections because your opposition is acting more like Jesus than ye who preach the gospel.

CHAPTER 8:

★ ★ ★

BLIND FAITH IN LIBERALISM

Did I just hear a gasp from the crowd when you read that chapter title? I think I did.

The extreme religious right believes that if you don't buy in to their political agenda, the odds are that you're headed to the H-E-double hockey sticks place. If you don't follow whichever sect of Christianity that they're a part of, then you're not in good shape. Odds are that you're a heathen, that you fornicate, willingly submit your body to drunkenness, and everything else that my father has told me I'm going to burn for (It's a long list). My faults aside, I want you to consider what's being said by Democrats and the left.

If you don't follow what they say blindly by accepting Obamacare, Russian collusion, social programs, or a lifestyle you may not agree with, then you're going to burn as well. Now it changes just a little from the religious right's message because the concept isn't about burning in hell, but rather being put under some sort of ultimate Nazi rule which makes literally no sense.

Rather than going on and on with the doctrine of the Bible, you're subjected to the doctrine of whichever politician is in charge. Right now, it's a bit of a stretch to see which Democrat is really in charge; it seems like we're still clinging to something in between Obama and Hillary Clinton, but it could just as easily be transferred over to anyone who pops up and has some sort of charisma that isn't named Bernie Sanders.

Didn't vote for Hillary Clinton? You hate women!

You're pro-life? You also hate women!

Don't want trans people to go to the bathroom they want to go into? You're a transphobe!

Don't Agree with the Obama on anything even though he's been proven wrong time and time again? You're racist!

See how fun and easy that is to do? It's basically the same thing that some extremists do on the right, except the answer to not agreeing with the religious people is hell.

Let's take a quick break to cool off from this very serious subject with a really fun dating story involving the term "homophobe," which, as you know, means the fear of gay people, but has been construed to mean hate of gay people:

I was on a date once with an incredibly attractive sociologist. You probably didn't need to know that she was incredibly attractive in order to get the gist of this story, but my ego needed stroking, so I threw that unnecessary detail in there.

We had gone to this little cute sushi place followed by a wine place on the water in Baltimore and were casually strolling back to her car. It was one of those moments when you knew that you could "get things going," with your date because things had gone incredibly well.

I had just put my arm around her and she started to ask me some of the most detailed sexual questions of my life. Now, I don't want to gross you out with all the details, but for those of you playing along at home, it involved my butt. Again, not to get into the gory details, but I had a lot of rapid-fire no questions that would have led any investigator to easily conclude that my butt is used for one of three things. Those things *only* include: sitting, shaking, and pooping. After the line of questions had ended, she stopped and stood as if to ponder what her next words would be. After the pause, she accused me of being homophobic.

I then spent the better part of the rest of our last date explaining to her that I was straight, hence why I was on the date with a woman, and that my lack of a desire to do anything with her that wasn't "vanilla" didn't make me homophobic. That, my friends, was the logic of a well-educated sociologist.

Just because you don't agree with someone doesn't mean that you hate them, a race, a sex, or an orientation. It just means you don't agree with someone, but that is the rhetoric that the left is being trained to drop on dissenters.

People are being asked to follow the left and all their principles blindly. Agree with everything in the liberal agenda or else you're a racist or you hate some type or class of person. That strategy makes perfect sense though. It's worked so far for Democrats, so why not crank up the volume even more?

CHAPTER 9:

★ ★ ★

DIFFERENT AGES, SIMILAR TRICKS

You know what holiday I love most? Actually it's two holidays that I love the most: Christmas and my birthday. I count my birthday as a holiday; you should as well. It's not just another day; it's a year closer to dying. Take some time off to do something on it.

Want to know why I love those two holidays? Those are the days that my family and friends get suckered in to giving me something that I have either requested or that they know that I already want. You have to love a scenario where you get something that you want or sometimes even need (like socks) for nothing! It's a great idea and everyone knows it. So why not manipulate the government so that people get things for free? That would certainly get you some votes, wouldn't it?

That's what the concept was under Franklin Delano Roosevelt. If you thought otherwise, you would be incorrect...I mean sure, people love to help out the elderly. Who doesn't (other than heartless bastards)? But we aren't typically heartless bastards. We like giving things to our grandparents. Politicians *really* love our grandparents, though; you know why?

They aren't distracted by the computers and the crappy television that the rest of us are hooked on. They came from the informed age of our nation and aren't even phased by our current information age well most of them aren't, I bet there are some grandparents who love them some internet porn. So guess what they all love doing? Voting!

Elderly people make up one of the largest and most consistent pools of people who not only register to vote, but actually go out and vote, so their votes are critical. How critical, you ask? So critical that smart regions of the country smack voting booths right in the lobby of the retirement homes. You can wheel your old folks right down the hallway to vote…they don't even have to leave their homes! How convenient! They're like double-guaranteed voting voters! So they are *super valuable* to any politician.

White gold I tells ya! White gold! Note: that white gold part isn't meant to be racist; it's actually referring to their old gray hair.

Politicians have known that the elderly have voted for years but both sides have handled it very differently.

The Democrats, starting with a huge bang under FDR, created the Social Security Administration, or SSA as us former employees of the place call it when we want to act smart. What was SSA created for? To hand out fat stacks to the elderly! To translate, "Handing out fat stacks," is hood-speak for "giving away tons of money."

And did that strategy ever work! Franklin Delano Roosevelt was known for a lot of things, one of them was the creation of SSA in 1935, and the other big one was that he was the only president to thwart the constitution and get elected for four terms. Now a lot of historians will say that this is because he was the president during World War II and to a point, I can't disagree with that. But you can bet your bottom dollar (I'm not sure what that means but I bet the government would take it) that handing out piles of money to the elderly didn't hurt his chances of that successful third election happening.

I know that a lot of people like to knock the Social Security Administration for their lack of accomplishments, slow pace, and for running out of money after being in business for almost eighty years. As someone who has worked at the Social Security Administration in two separate tours as a graduate intern, I can tell you this: all the criticisms are absolutely true.

I'm not sure how the Social Security Administration grew to the level that it has gotten to, but it's completely out of hand. Jobs as SSA are wonderful and should be considered an immediate retirement from normal working life once you're accepted into the fold. On the main campus in Woodlawn, there is a full gym, fantastic cafeteria, great lounges to hang out in, and even a Maryland Lottery store. It was like getting paid to go to a country club every single morning when I woke up.

To be honest with you, I think they made them shut down the lottery store because too many people were busy playing scratch-offs instead of not working at their desks and it became annoying to the higher ups. When you aren't playing your birthday at the lottery machines, you could go to one of many of the general stores and buy snacks or get this…full novels. Don't want to gamble, read, or snack? That's okay; there's a full-time gym running on campus as well. Sure it costs a bit each month to join, but if you buy a package where you work out during off-peak hours, instead of peak, you'll save money. That's right: if you work out during the middle of the workday, rather than during lunch or before or after the normal before 8:30 AM or after 5 PM time, you'll save money.

What a great place to "work!"

I was especially skilled when I was there with a law education and graduate public policy work under my belt; I got to work with some top policy-making divisions. So my job included responding to audits once in a while that questioned why we needed to spend four hundred dollars on brownies at conferences. Duh…education. You need super delicious brownie carbs to get educated by SSA! Stupid auditors.

The greatest experience I had there though, and the most telling, was when I was working on a project that could have helped the government save millions of dollars from slipping through the cracks of SSA. I was tasked to do some initial research on essentially helping the government stop fraud from happening with our systems. The task and research was expected to take me about a month. I accomplished the entire project in under half a day. I guess I did something wrong by being efficient there, so I was called into my boss's office.

My boss: "Tim, I wanted to speak to you today about your work here in the office."

Me, a bit scared: "Okay, is everything okay?"

My boss: "Yes and no. See, a couple of your coworkers came to me and complained about you the other day. And I know this is going to be confusing to you, but can you please slow down the pace of your work?"

Me, feeling a bit relieved of my initial fear, but now confused: "Slow down my pace?"

My boss: "Yes, see you've been completing projects at a much faster pace than many of your coworkers are familiar with, so if you could please slow it down, that would be great."

Me, holding back laughter: "How do I do that?"

My boss: "Well look, you know when meetings are, so just take breaks and go do whatever. Just make sure you make it to meetings."

That happened.

I should've been more shocked by that conversation. I probably should have been appalled, but instead I took it with a grain of salt and went to work on a plan. I was wrapping up law school and had begun working on a doctorate in Public Policy simultaneously, so I started completing homework and reading at my desk. When that wasn't enough to hold over my time, I started eBay-ing. I developed what I call now my eBay problem during that time. I was spending too much money online while sitting bored at my desk. In that semester alone, I pieced together the entire five hundred home run hitter club autographs, except for Babe Ruth and two other guys whose autographs are valued in the thousands of dollars. I actually spent so much money on eBay that I realized it wasn't fun anymore. So I set my eBay spending rates to two hundred dollars a week tops in order to complete the collection. That still wasn't enough to feed my boredom.

So in a last ditch effort to stay busy—keep in mind I was completing homework and reading for law school; wandering campus and meeting new friends (I thought that would be assumed already); and eBay-ing what is now an incredible collection of baseball autographs for a fraction of their value—I broke down and started paying to download full seasons of my favorite TV show, *Scrubs*, to watch at my desk. All that, my friends, and I was still completing my work at a pace that beat most of my coworkers at SSA.

So when someone doesn't believe that the Social Security Administration was created simply to hand old people money in exchange for votes, I laugh in their faces.

Old people are critical to campaigns for more than just votes though. Not only do they get money from the government, but they also have the money to give to campaigns. This just gets sweeter and sweeter for politicians, doesn't it?

After all those years of hard work, what's left for the elderly to do, especially the successful ones? Travel and influence future generations. And what better way to do that than by dropping coin on campaigns? Actually, there is a better way to influence future generations, and that happens to be donating money to the "Tim Young Needs Your Money Campaign" or TYNYMC; I am always open to taking money off your hands in order to help better the world in ways that only I can. My live jokes don't pay for themselves, people, and you can rest assured knowing that all proceeds will go to pay off my student loans, then pay off the debt incurred by creating one of the greatest baseball autograph collections of all time.

Where was I? Oh yes, old people have money to give! So of course there are going to be plenty of advocates and entertainment rolled out for the older, richer folks. Need an example? Barbara Streisand on the left! Need an example on the right? Well, they are kind of lacking in celebrities, but they have that figure skating guy who would do the flip on the ice that my mom loves! Oh that guy is awesome! He did ice skating at the Olympics and stuff and then on TV on Saturday mornings when I was younger and wanted to watch WWE Superstars, but *Stars on Ice* was on and Mom had the remote. He's the Republicans' guy! They also have that group that sings "Elvira," but they never sing "Elvira" when I see them at charity events. I don't have time to write out everyone, so for a complete list of all the celebrities that the left can pull out to entertain old people, just Google, "Old people celebrities," and just assume all of those results.

Guess what else old people love doing? They *love* going to church! And as if they aren't already a lock on voting, wanna take another guess at what other group of people consistently register to vote and then actually go out and vote? Churchgoers!

Here is where I have a problem with any politician on either side of the aisle. The separation of "state and church." I say state and church rather than church and state because in my book, it's two completely separate things. The separation of state and church is when a politician goes and speaks in a church to drum up votes and support. I think it's wrong to do. A lot of Republicans disagree with me on this point, probably because they want to throw their candidate in front of a church or are that candidate who goes and speaks at a church about politics.

The reason that I don't think politicians should speak in front of a church is simple: it's unfairly persuasive. People who attend church have faith in God. Absolute faith in something they can't see, hear, feel or touch. They just believe in God and believe that He's there for them. What they are learning on a Sunday or a Wednesday or whichever day they decide to attend church is what they have blind faith in. That's not a bad thing at all. What is bad, however, is when you interject someone who is there for selfish reasons to speak in front of people who are there based on faith. See where this is going?

What happens when a politician speaks from a pulpit on a day of worship is that those same people who typically believe everything that comes from that same pulpit any other Sunday will misplace their faith in God and their church and believe anything that the person who wants them to put him in power will say to him. It's a dangerous position to put your congregation in, especially when they are there to learn and love God, not learn from and love a politician.

When I say separation of state and church, I limit it though to that pulpit on a day of worship. If that politician wants to throw the church a cookout after service or visit them at an off-campus event, I don't have a problem with it. But standing in front of a church on a day of worship is manipulation of someone's faith.

I was asked to give a communion meditation back in high school at my church. For those of you who don't know what that is, it's when you go and give some thoughts about Jesus and the Bible before you pass out the wine/grape juice and the crackers or whatever bread substance your church uses to symbolize Jesus. I was nervous but confident that my comparison of our lives as Christians to that of a Klingon warrior from *Star Trek: The Next Generation* would have really touched some hearts. Shockingly, I was never invited to give a communion meditation again in front of a church. I really thought they would have eaten that up.

In comparison, my church frequently invited a Republican ~~politician joker~~ hypocrite to come and speak repeatedly about his good works in our state's capitol and what he would do to uphold Christianity for everyone in the world or something.... Needless to say, he was elected multiple times and went on to get arrested for drunk driving a boat and has been accused of many more things along the way!

He was allowed to speak in front of a church, claiming to be as Christian as everyone else, and went on to be a mess...but our church helped elect him!

If a church elects to bring a politician in to their congregation who also wasn't already a member, I don't see why they can't give his competitor the same amount of time. If there's an equal time doctrine requiring all media stations that have one politico on to have their opposition on during a campaign season to keep it fair, there should also be one for churches. Again, if you're going to allow your body of believers to hear from an ambitious person who wants political power, you should allow them to hear from them fairly. That would eliminate what I call the issue of state and church. But what are the odds of that actually happening?

Sometimes we even go as far as to memorialize our elders. They typically deserve it, but the best is when our politicians use those memorials to manipulate our older population, you know, like when Democrats decide that national memorials for Vietnam and World War II are non-essential government programs and decide to close public space to the public.

Remember the GOP holdout and government shutdown a few years ago under Obama? Obama didn't have to, but he shut down parks, museums, and memorials as a strategy to anger the elderly (and the regular public, but mainly the elderly—let's face it: they're basically the ones who go to those things). After all, old people love that stuff! So while the media was spinning their wheels trying to find new ways to blame Republicans for that government shutdown, Obama thought to add his own exclamation point to the issue by closing everything old people love! Free museums, memorials dedicated to them, and parks...you know, stuff young people don't really have the time for anymore.

Did that backfire? Maybe at the time. I know most of the Republican House Members went down to help our brave World War II vets to get into the memorials after all, but for the most part, people were pissed off that the right was the reason it was shut down.... After all, it was what we were told to believe, so most of us believed it.

Some people could call what the Democrats do good ole manipulation of the elderly, but I don't. I think it's just smart politics. We all know what old people want; it's just that the Democrats for years played their cards better with the older population than Republicans did. Not only that, but the Republicans just let them do it! It's like the GOP watches as the Democrats create programs and give out everything but free lunches...and sometimes even that... to the older generation and did *nothing about it.*

At least call them out on what's going on, right? We can't just sit back and wait for the old people to die off. They're going to be kindly rolled down the hallways of their nursing homes to their voting booths then rolled right back every election, and unless we stand up and start really calling out the left on their basic manipulations, this will continue to happen. Thank God that the left also doesn't do a good job at getting young people out to vote...oh wait, they do.

CHAPTER 10:

★ ★ ★

CHANGE THE VOTING AGE FROM 18 TO WHICHEVER AGE IT IS WHEN PEOPLE GAIN COMMON SENSE

A few years ago, young people *finally* decided to start showing up to the polls and guess why? Barack Obama!

Well maybe not Barack Obama, but they were finally excited enough to vote in elections for some reason or another that has to do with Democrats!

Here's the deal: young people didn't used to vote. They didn't. Why? Because well, maybe some of them were too stupid to register to vote before election day in 2000 when they had the first opportunity of their lives to vote in a presidential election. Or if you aren't me, it's because voting in elections takes time to get off your lazy butt and wait in line with a bunch of people who were just rolled to the polling place in their wheelchair smelling like mothballs.

And the last thing that young people want is to go home smelling like mothballs.

When you're young, you just don't realize how important things are and you have other things to distract you, you know, like Demi Lovato and video games and Facebook and Demi Lovato. You know, if for some reasons someone starts reading this book even five years in the future, they'll put it down as soon as they reach a dated Demi

Lovato reference. So just for consistency's sake, in 2018, she didn't look like she does now, people of the future.

Young people just have other stuff to do that is more exciting than voting. Now I know what some young people who read this book are going to say, "There's nothing more important than voting!" They're going to declare it with an exclamation point too... but you, my friends, are smarter than that. For example, if I at twenty (nerdy, lonely, awkward, and nearly 320 pounds) was offered sex for the first time in my life with a girl I was dating in exchange for not voting, I would not have voted. Sorry, Republican Party; I would have passed on voting for sex. At twenty-two, that offer of sex could wait 'til the afternoon after I got my "I voted" sticker. That's where my logic was at twenty and twenty-two; it made a world of difference.

For some young people nowadays, it doesn't even take that much effort to get them to not vote. It really comes down to an emotional level for them, do they care or not. Want to know how to make them care? Just watch at what the Democrats pulled a few years ago in 2012...and watch it good.

"How many of you know someone who is gay?" was probably one of the best taglines of the entire campaign...but I'm getting ahead of myself. Let's start from the very beginning.

What does your life consist of at eighteen? For the most part at eighteen years old, you still have no clue who you are. Case in point? Me.

At eighteen, I was valedictorian, head of all sorts of clubs, a virgin, had just received a full scholarship to go to college to pursue the perfect job: biochemical engineer. What the fuck was I thinking? At that point in my life, I had barely been lucky enough to get one woman to date me, She was essentially Blossom from the eponymous show, without any of the good qualities of Blossom.

The *best* part about being eighteen? I had a safety net called my parents' house! If things failed, my parents would have helped me out...what a sweet deal!

Let's see where Tim Young went four years later.

At twenty-two, I had no clue what a biochemical engineer was and never wanted to know what that was. To this day, if you're a biochemical engineer, God bless you and your contributions to society, but don't ever bore me to death by telling me what terrible stuff you do at your job—unless you're the bioengineer who makes up Jelly Belly flavors (I saw it on *Dirty Jobs* once, so now I'm an expert at that one specific person does). I was in only one club in college, the Student Government Association, while interning on Capitol Hill learning how to write policy. I was dating a former Redskinette (those are cheerleaders for the Washington football team that liberals always hate the name of) who was nowhere near as intelligent as the girl from high school even after four years of college, and who had just cheated on me. She devastated my very small world at the time. I had ballooned up to the size of that morbidly obese bunny rabbit, having gained seventy-five pounds in the time between these relationships.

The *worst* part about being twenty-two? Even though I still had that safety net, because my parents were still there for me at that point in my life, I would've felt terrible having to move home again and have them do so. It would be taking advantage of things if I did that and had a real job.

The game of life had changed.

I was a completely different person with actual tangible knowledge of the world. I wouldn't miss the opportunity to vote again if you paid me a significant amount of money *and* offered me sex from some other dumb Redskinette!

So what would have gotten my blood boiling enough at eighteen to get me voting? Not much. Life is good at eighteen. You'd have to really piss me off in order to get me out and voting. I mean, you would have to do something that hit home, like threaten my friends' way of life.

Bingo!

Democrats hit the nail right on the head with this one. So let's revisit that question from before:

"How many of you know someone who is gay?"

By the time you're eighteen and in modern society, aka anyone who didn't attend a Christian school—because if the kids are gay at Christian school, they're probably going to hide it out of fear—knows someone who's gay!

"Well guess what's going to happen if Republicans win this time?"

The media basically tells us that they're going to kill all the gays! The GOP is going to round them all up in buses and ship them to detention centers. After they burn all the rainbow flags, they're going to burn every one of your gay friends at the stake or have Michelle Bachmann's husband convert them back to being straight—whichever happens first.

They might as well have said that. We suddenly had everyone in Hollywood telling us that you're a homophobe if you don't want to let gay people get married—and this was years before Trump time. You're just a hating hater who hates things that are just going to happen anyway, you hating hater. And do you know who hates gay people the most? Republicans. But do you know who loves gay people to the point that they would totally marry them if they were gay? Democrats.

If you're eighteen, have no life experience, and have a gay friend, that message not only convinced you to vote, it convinced to vote Democrat. The worst part was that the GOP didn't fight back.

Wait, so you're one of the few kids out there from those remote schools that didn't know any gay people growing up? That message wasn't going to hit you over the head to drag you out to the polls; they needed something worse.

"Hey, eighteen-year-olds! How many of you know women?" was the very next question.

"Holy crap! I know a woman!" excitedly replies impressionable eighteen-year old me.

"You do? Well guess what's going to happen if Republicans win this time?"

It's going to be *The Handmaid's Tale!* The GOP are going to take charge of women's healthcare the old-fashioned way: by personally overseeing every procedure a woman has done on her body in the capacity of self-appointed medical doctors. They think they have the rights to stop women from having abortions, because you know when women need abortions? All the time. And when a woman has sex and needs an abortion because she won't want to be responsible for kids, it's going to be the Republicans' fault if she can't have one.

Eighteen-year old Tim just signed up to vote in the 2000 election for Al Gore to make sure that that would never happen.

That's basically how things are spun for kids at eighteen. Remember the old telephone game, where you would start by whispering "I love eating spaghetti," into your classmate's ear in kindergarten and by the end, it came out something like, "teaspoons and peanut butter jelly"? That's exactly what would happen here, except the message started off with something more along the lines of "Republicans hate women and gays," and evolved into those long *crazy* paragraphs that we saw above.

Once you got the kids' attention with "Republicans want to terminate your friends and family," they start actually listening to lines like "This is the most important election of our lifetime," and realizing that their free The Black Eyed Peas concert was only free because Democrats made that happen. Add that in with the fact that Republicans did *nothing* to counter this and Democrats have *mastered the internet* and you've got the perfect storm to get young people out to vote.

Don't worry; we'll get to the utter hypocrisy of Democrats' gay and women loving later. And yes, we're also going to cover how Al Gore didn't create the internet, but the Barack Obama campaign damn near took over the entire internet/email world with what they did, but first, let's talk about how Republicans lost the fight for young people in 2012.

THE REPUBLICAN PARTY DID NOTHING SIGNIFICANT TO FIGHT FOR YOUNG VOTERS IN 2012

Well, now that we covered that base…

The GOP did nothing to attract young voters to counteract the Democrats emotional appeal to young people in 2012. Nothing.

Paul Ryan. He's young…ish. He drove the Oscar Meyer Weinermobile when he was a kid; he also lightly worked out during a photo shoot. That's what young people got.

"Come on, Republican strategists; you've got to have something better than that!" I yelled. It turned out that they didn't.

The left had all the big celebrities, they had Hollywood, and they had pop music, the combination of which basically make up everything and anything that a young person cares about. Couple that with big scary messages about how the right wants to destroy your friends and family, and guess what's going to happen?

Four more years of Barack Obama.

The numbers here didn't lie. Barack Obama got young people to vote based on those facts alone…

But wait, there's *more*!

How soon we forget that basically every level of education—graduate school, undergrad, high school, middle school, elementary school, and even that wacky *Yo Gabba Gabba* garbage that I don't understand how anyone could even watch for more than fifteen seconds—are dominated by the left.

No one will deny that the entire education system is comprised of progressives, even further left progressives, and hippies who are lucky that some institutionalized education programs don't drug test. It's common knowledge.

What recent teacher's union has ever supported a Republican candidate? Seriously. I would say that there might be one if the Christian schools worked via our socialist union system, but they're smart enough not to do that. So here's what I'll do if you can prove me wrong. I'll give you a prize. If you can name one, send a self-addressed stamped envelope to:

The I Found a Non-Liberal Teachers Union Foundation
c/o Tim Young
1234 No You Didn't You Lying Bag of Crap Avenue
Washington, DC 20001

Your prize? An unquestionably warm joy knowing that you just threw money into a dying United States Postal Service.

It doesn't matter where you go or what you do in education; you're going to run into the left. I *love* the fact that we still say teachers should be paid more. *Love it*. It's complete union derived spin.

Now before you start thinking that I would say the same about cops and firemen, you're wrong. Those guys and gals literally put their lives on the line every single day for us out there. In one second, a police officer or fireman could lose their lives, when their entire job is to protect us by putting their lives on the line. Teachers…have it easy compared to them.

My friends who are in education always try to argue this with me, but they always end up shutting up because I'm right on the subject. Teachers have it rough for a bit. They have to come up with a yearlong set of lesson plans, which is taxing for their first year. That isn't fun, but if they teach the same subject for the rest of their career, all they have to do is alter that extreme amount of work a little bit each year and they're set. That's a pretty sweet deal. In fact, I'm going to take a page straight out of their books; when I'm finished writing this pile of words that we've all somehow agreed is a book, I'm going to change a couple of the words and chapter titles and call it a completely new book, then demand more money for it!

Sound fair to you? No?

Here's the next great part about being a teacher. You only work nine months out of the year! How many of us would love to have the same schedule we had when we went to school? We got a week off for Thanksgiving! *Thanksgiving*! Do you know how much shopping we could get done during that time? Then we got a week for Christmas and New Year's and then *spring break*!

What exactly is spring break? What is the purpose of having a week off in the middle of the spring? Seriously. But teachers get it. I feel like I'm forgetting something else…oh yes:

Teachers have the entire summer off!

Now I know some teachers say they have to start going back and decorating bulletin boards and have a couple of meetings here and there over the summer but *come on!* You have months off! If you were paid, say, an extra 33 percent of your salary, which after tricky math, makes up for those three months off, that would be great, but no! You get paid enough. There are also lots of scholarships and incentives like fancy state-provided healthcare and retirement that you get that us common people can't touch. You're doing well, teachers. So stop toeing the union line.

I love teachers; don't get me wrong. If it weren't for the ones I had throughout my academic career, I wouldn't be as knowledgeable as I am now, nor would I have been able to accomplish all that I have in life—but no more money for you. You're doing okay.

College professors are typically much worse and much more liberal. Here is where you can see some of the craziest stuff around. Let's start with where the education is coming from and what it's like to be in a doctoral program. I and many of my friends went through one, so I know. When you're in academia, you're in a world of your own. Now when I refer to academia, you should know that I'm talking about academic graduate programs that aren't taught functionally. Business school, law school, and specific schools which are taught using real world examples are functional schools. Want to learn how to lock up a criminal or sue somebody? Go to law school. Want to learn how to sell crap to people? Go to business school. Want to learn the theory behind why when your children act out we shouldn't spank them or else they'll end up with a mental disorder that we've only proven to exist in 2 percent of the population of Zambia? Go to graduate school for psychology, sociology, or something else that someone has made up.

Side note: you can actually go to school to get a doctorate in sexology. It's a thing. I sat next to a woman on a plane who was a registered sexologist once. They literally study the theories of what makes people freaks. I'd love to say it would be more than that, but people know how sex works; they just increase the study of why people like to hug teddy bears and cry when they do it. They also design condoms. I don't think a normal person could survive going a week in a sexology school. And I, being the idiot that I am, thought to myself "Sexologist?! That must mean like a stripper or porn star." I never said I was classy. I'm a typical guy once in a while., "I should ask her out! What could possibly go wrong?" Sexologists are just the same as any other academic. They're boring and come from a sheltered land comprised of sheltered, equal minded people.

Let's talk about those sheltered people from a sheltered land, shall we?

First of all, the reason I went to graduate school to get a doctorate in public policy was twofold: first, I thought Doctor Young, JD, PhD had a great ring to it. If there were literally more letters around my name than in my name, people would *have* to listen to my terrible rantings at that point, right?

Second: the doctorate was a combined program of law school and grad school. I technically started in my second or third year of a four-year doctoral program with my law degree. Who could turn down a deal like that?

I will never forget sitting down with my law school's academic advisor to discuss getting the paperwork together to get into the program.Keep in mind that law school is a functional school. She turned to me and said, "You know you're only the second person in this school's history to attempt this, right? The other one never finished."

I felt extremely proud at that moment. I was already the first person in my family to go to college and law school, and now I was going to be the first person in the school's history to get a combined law degree and doctorate in public policy! I was going to be a torchbearer for the world with this, or something.

"You're not going to finish the program," she continued.

"Why?" I immediately shot back, "This seems like an incredible opportunity."

"You're going to hate it. I know you're going to hate it, and not just because the last person who tried it hated it, but I know you. You aren't going to like the people there. I'm not saying they aren't nice, but you aren't going to like the people, you aren't going to like the pace, you aren't going to like the subjects…. The people are weird, the subjects are hokey compared to law school, and if you thought professors were political here, you're going to be blown away by professors in a doctoral program. Here we live for functionality and we're hard on you so you learn. There, they're going to be hard on you just because they're hard on you to prove they're better. And wait 'til they find out that you're a Republican. You just…aren't…going…to…like…it."

"Whatever," I thought to myself. "I'm a champion of education and the world; I'll be able to handle them and it'll end up like some sort of grand movie about academics where we all learn to love and grow from each other."

Roughly twenty-five thousand dollars and a year and a half later, I realized she was absolutely correct. The only people I got along with in the program were people who already had careers and were literally only there to complete a program to get an automatic raise at work. Everyone else for the most part just seemed to live in a world of his or her own. Some established professors were great too—don't get me wrong; there are always outliers—but for the most part, it was a nightmare. The best part is that a lot of these sheltered folks who do nothing but learn about their favorite subjects and sleep from other people who only learned about their same favorite topics and slept were their insane personalities.

Here's a great example of a graduate student that was in my public policy program, a thought leader whose writings I'm sure will one day be quoted as they work to make the world significantly more progressive.

I won't release her name, but we'll call her Janice, just for a point of reference. Janice identified herself as a progressive. She would do nothing but drink, go to class, do graduate assistant work, and sleep. So far, so good, right? Just a normal graduate student. Janice grew up in the northeast to a filthy rich family and attended a very high-end private university there as well. Don't get me wrong here; I'm not knocking high-end private universities; I'm just building her character. Some of you on the right were going to start grumbling by merely hearing that she attended a northeastern private university...don't.

Here's where it gets fun...

Every night in class at 7:30 PM, she would bring in a fifteen-course meal, including, but not limited to, a small can of Pringles, cheese doodles, two pudding cups, and her toes. I'm not going to mock her size because I've had weight issues, but I knew when I was bigger to look in a mirror and not wear shirts that were so tight that they would show every roll in my body and come up over my belly, not to show midriff, but rather because it was out of surface area that it could cover.

I never knew of anyone who would lick the inside of a Pringles can to get all of the flavor crystals out, but she did. Crystal by crystal, salt grain by salt grain, we watched her extend her Gene Simmons-esque tongue into the can and seemingly touch every one on a forty-five degree angle in the air from her front row center seat in the middle of class. This would continue on every class that we had together that night of the week. First it was Pringles, then it was cheese doodles which she would slowly chew down from that same angle, like a baby bird receiving pre-chewed food from its mother. She would next slowly lick off every bit of the orange from her fingertips. After that, it was on to pudding cups one and then two. And, you guessed it, after significant scraping with a spoon, it was back up to that forty-five degree angle to lick out what was left.

And just when you thought the party had ended, she started scraping her fingers in between each of her shoeless toes and putting whatever she found into her mouth. Once a month, we would even get treated to her clipping her toenails to go with it. She didn't eat those, though.

Feel sick yet?

Now imagine that thought leader turning to me to argue a political point and having a *really* disgusting uppity attitude about why she was right. In addition to her disgusting habits, she was just a disgusting person. She was mean, arrogant, and did I mention never wrong? *Never* wrong. Her opinions on things were so staunch because everyone around her in her life until that moment told her she was right; she didn't have the time to listen to anything that could be considered different from her. If you had a different opinion, you were automatically wrong. If that different opinion continued to hold weight in the conversation, then you were only arguing with her because she was a woman and you clearly didn't respect women or thought that women weren't as smart as men.

That's who's going to be teaching your children.

Look, I do a lot of disgusting things, but at least I know social norms and can hold it back…or not hold it back when I want to.

Progressive professors aren't the smartest, though, and I used that to my advantage somewhere in between that carrying the torch to be the first JD/PhD combined program graduate and saying "Screw this program and these people."

See, as smart as the sheltered people in a sheltered land are, if you can sound like you're smarter, or on "their level," you'll win. The best example of this was when I was writing a ridiculously long research paper in a political science theory class. See, because public policy and its theories are basically a modern science, most of the "thought leaders" in the subject are still alive. I was sick of reading at that point. Between everything that I had just gone through in law school reading policy and the legal cases, then on to reading basically garbage from theorists in class for ridiculously long discussions that led nowhere in graduate school, I was over it. So I thought to myself, "If this guy is alive, why don't I just call him and get him to basically dictate new theory to me, essentially writing my entire paper?" That's exactly what I did.

I called up said theorist and after his I kid you not, morning stroll through the fields of his northeastern university, he called me right back. We discussed his forthcoming works over a thirty-five-minute phone call and I wrote a roughly twenty-five-page research paper (with pictures!) about our conversation. My references in the paper were our phone conversation, his forthcoming works, and his telephone number. I gamed the progressive education system.

Even that got old after a while. Professors would argue with me to argue with me in class. They didn't like how I dressed (I still love crappy logo t-shirts, jeans, and jerseys), they didn't like my politics, and in the end they didn't even like what I was going to propose as a dissertation (a fluid model of the economic impact of Supreme Court decisions...*boring*!) so I left the program and went on to make money in the real world.

The reason I share those stories with you is because I want you to know what academia is like. I have a feeling that most academics would argue with me about their specific program or their colleagues' behavior, but people who are in grad school know that my stories could probably be replicated at almost every school. See, if I were Janice, I probably would have had no issues graduating from the program because I was of the same mind as everyone else there. Sure, I would have no knowledge of social norms and be a relatively disgusting and closed-minded person, but I'd still be there. Because I was of different thoughts and a different political persuasion, things were made more difficult for me as if it were some higher-level political game.

And these are the people teaching our children.

Let's look at what's happened here to young people.

First, they're getting angry because they are being told in one way or another that Republicans hate and want to destroy their friends' way of life; next they're being taught by progressives all the way through their academic careers. And those progressives know only three things: 1) they love the left; 2) their academic area of expertise; and 3) anyone other than them is wrong for one reason or another. Republicans have just lost the battle for young people because again:

REPUBLICANS HAVE DONE NOTHING SIGNIF-ICANT TO FIGHT FOR YOUNG VOTERS.

Remember how I mentioned earlier that eighteen-year-olds basically only care about a few things? Entertainment was one of them. It's not like young people would be trained by the left all the way through their childhoods to think a certain way—you know, like guns are bad or something?—to take our Second Amendment rights, right?

Now before I get into it here, I don't want you to think that I wear a tinfoil hat and believe that there is a vast left-wing conspiracy to take our guns. I don't believe that at all. In fact, that is crazy talk. The fact is that the left doesn't want people to have guns, and they are working on creating legislation to take guns away. What they are not doing is creating a grand scheme that would brainwash people into thinking that guns are bad and could ruin lives. The fact is that they don't need to because the groundwork has already inadvertently been put there by Hollywood.

You just have to think of who is creating the media that young people are paying attention to. It's left-minded people. And left-minded people just aren't fans of guns. Ever since I can remember throughout my childhood and growing up, I have been trained to think that guns are bad things. This might be because of the type of television I watched, it might also be because I grew up in southwest Baltimore, which is one of the bluest regions of the country. Either way, I was taught that guns are bad.

Without getting into the Second Amendment here, let's just talk about what media I was presented growing up.

The first thing I learned as a kid from media was that gun owners are idiots and rednecks. Things are spun to say people who own guns have no idea what they're doing with their weapons and that they cause more harm than good by simply owning something with which to protect themselves.

It is difficult to find television characters who aren't police officers or "bad guys," who openly carry guns. Don't let this take up more of your time then necessary. There has been a recent trend with more heroes, particularly in comic-book-based television, but before comic books were everywhere, the only exception was in my guilty pleasure cartoon, *Justice League Unlimited* (I own all the good guy action figures by the way) where there was a character named Vigilante who not only carried six-shooters, but also shot at bad guys. He did kind of fit the stereotype though, because he was a southern redneck who wore a cowboy hat and covered his face with a kerchief like a western villain. That is literally the only exception. The rest of the children's shows I watched went more like an episode of *The Simpsons* I saw years ago.

Did you ever see the one where Homer decided to buy a gun? That stereotypical idiot used that weapon for everything from opening a beer can to drink out of to changing the channel on the television. He was shooting it everywhere and at everything, destroying his house and neighborhood until we were all taught the lesson that guns are the worst possible thing that you could ever buy.

I hate to admit it, but I also *watched Mighty Morphin' Power Rangers* as a teenager. I think the target demographic for the program was below twelve, but I was okay watching it at sixteen; it wasn't like I had a social life to worry about. As a not-so-dumb sixteen-year-old, I remember being befuddled by the fact that the rangers wouldn't use their guns in defense when monsters with super powers were attacking them. They literally had guns in holsters on their side and were getting torn apart by monsters double their size attempting to take them on in them hand-to-hand combat. It. Made. No. Sense.

Just think about what Americans are shown on television and in movies. Guns are rarely used in a positive way unless it's a hunting show or law enforcement is handling them. Even then, we see officers shy away from guns or get admonished if their guns are fired.

Some of you may even be familiar with the television show *Flashpoint*, about a tactical team that takes out criminals via sniper rifle and other methods of gun use. On its face, the show appears to shed positive light on gun ownership, but that is not the case.

David Paetkau, who was a regular on the show, was once quoted in an interview by Coast Reporter as saying that *Flashpoint*, "tries to capture the human element involved in policing and discusses how some officers end up with emotional baggage and suffering with mental illnesses like post traumatic stress disorder."

See? Hollywood tells us yet again that if you use a gun even in protecting people and saving the world, you are going to be mentally ill or have some sort of issue.

Now don't get confused by what I just said. I'm going to re-iterate again that I don't at all believe that there is some large conspiracy to take our guns. I don't think Hollywood is planting government-directed messages into young people's brains. What I am saying here is that there are clowns to the left of them; jokers to the right, and there young people are: stuck in the middle.

Young people are being manipulated by the politicians and strategists on the left; they are being manipulated to think progressively by the educators; and they are being manipulated to think progressively by Hollywood. And what has the right done to counteract this? What have they done to help young people and get them away from all of this left-wing influence? Wait for it; I think I have it queued up in my cut and paste by now.

REPUBLICANS HAVE DONE NOTHING SIGNIFICANT TO FIGHT FOR YOUNG VOTERS.

So as much as you might hate the left for manipulating young people, you should hate the right for doing nothing to stop them.

★ ★ ★

CHAPTER 11

HEY, REPUBLICANS: MINORITIES HATE YOU FOR A REASON

Have you ever wondered why minorities don't vote for Republicans? You should. It's really curious if you think about it.

It is so tricky for a white guy who has already declared himself a Republican in a book to speak about race. I can see through this book already a bunch of folks who have grabbed a highlighter and popped the cap off with their teeth, just waiting for the moment to scream that I'm a racist or said something racist. Here, you won't find it. I take race and politics more seriously than any other subject because it's close to my heart. Let's cover a few background points on me before we really get into this.

When I perform on stage, I love talking about how I grew up in the hood in Baltimore. More specifically, I grew up down the street from a *Colt 45* malt liquor plant. I didn't just grow up in a hood; I grew up in the hood that helped create and maintain other hoods around this great nation.

A lot of my good friends are minorities, and when I say minorities, I don't mean just black. I have black, Asian, Hispanic, Native American, and everything-else-in-between friends…and unlike people who use this excuse as a cover for being discriminatory, I have more friends than you can count on one hand. There hasn't been a single time when I have heard someone being accused of being racist that they don't automatically come back with, "But I have (whatever race you're being accused of not liking) friends!" Just a quick FYI, that pretty much puts an exclamation point on your being racist at this point.

It's like the lonely single person saying they have a boyfriend or girlfriend, but no one ever sees them because they're, "always so busy," or "out of the country."

When I grew up in the 1980s in Baltimore, neither I nor most of my friends saw race as an issue. We were all relatively poor kids growing in a not-so good part of town. When I graduated high school, I was informed by administration and the PTA statistics that our school was the highest in the county in narcotics and teen pregnancy.

I understand poverty because at every point in my childhood, someone around me, if not me, was living in it. No one was mocked for being on the school lunch program as a kid. In fact, I thought it was cool that a good chunk of my friends got to trade in tickets for their food rather than having to pay for it. I just didn't know any better.

We grew together as a community and for the most part, we supported each other as a community.

This is me with Al Sharpton. He was not thrilled to take this picture with me.

One of the funniest things that happened to me growing up in Baltimore was when I was chosen in third grade to play Doctor Martin Luther King Jr. in the Martin Luther King Day celebration at my elementary school. It made no sense and to this day, my parents still remind me of it. How can I forget when I was chosen by my African American teacher over a wide selection of black students to play the civil rights icon? Again, none of the children saw anything wrong with this. When I got older, I realized it was kind of messed up that I was picked to play him when there were other less incredibly white kids to choose from, but it was I who read the "I Have a Dream," speech to the entire school. Could you imagine if that happened in today's world?

There would have been protests and outrage in the streets that the whitest white boy in the entire school was chosen to play Doctor King on his day! I'm actually kind of shocked that there weren't protests then, but hey, I guess people really weren't as sensitive in the 1980s.

I mentioned my full ride to college earlier on. The original scholarship that I received was socio-economic and minority based. I'll never forget some of the reactions of the students that I was up against to get into the program during what was called "selection weekend." During the weekend, we went through a series of interviews and a process to prove that we were worthy of the scholarship. The candidates for the program were comprised of some of the smartest people I have ever met in my life, but more importantly for me, all of those candidates, except for a tiny handful, were African American.

For the very first time in my life, I was a minority as a white guy. This might also be the *only* time I was a minority in any scenario in my life if you don't count times I've performed at urban comedy clubs. I remember being asked in our three-on-one personal interview why a program like this was so important. My response, "People from different cultures bring different perspectives to the table. This program allows people who may not have a chance to come to college to get that opportunity. It also allows those different perspectives to contribute to professions where they may never have been heard before. In essence, what's happening here is that you're providing an opportunity to individuals of different cultures and upbringings so that they will then enrich the world with their different heritage."

Sounds pretty progressive coming from a white male Republican, doesn't it? But that wasn't coming from a white male Republican.... That was coming from a poor kid who was taught that he had the power to change the world and knew that without a scholarship, he wouldn't be able to have that chance.

Those aren't liberal or conservative thoughts. That wasn't a Democrat or a Republican speaking. That was a human being who believed that he could make a difference and knew that other people needed to have that same chance.

The magic of all the race and diversity talk is that it boils down to just plain not understanding one another. Over the next four years of college, those incredibly intelligent black students I had met during that weekend became my friends and those friends all for the most part went on to become doctors and researchers who changed the world. They were also some of the greatest teachers I had ever had.

I learned about a lot of stuff that my Republican friends have called excuses and false claims about racism in America. Those same Republican friends of mine refuse to take the time to learn from minorities and those that are different from them. That might be a bit of a clue as to why over 80 percent of the Hispanic, Asian and Black populations in America voted for Barack Obama in the 2012 election. Just a bit though...Let's start our history lesson on race and politics, shall we?

There are three facts about Republicans that we get thrown into our faces during every election cycle:

1. Republicans under Abraham Lincoln freed the slaves. That includes ratifying the Fourteenth and Fifteenth Amendments to the Constitution, making slaves legal citizens and giving them the right to vote.

2. Republicans helped found the NAACP. That's right. That's a fact. The Grand Old Party helped form the National Association for the Advancement of Colored People.

3. Republicans worked with forward-thinking Democrats to squash Southern Democrats and end racial segregation in this country. In fact, a higher percentage of Republicans than Democrats in both houses of Congress voted to desegregate the country.

As a Republican, I'm extremely proud of those facts. But can I ask a quick question? *What in the blue hell has happened since then?*

How can a political party that has been so successful in civil rights go from all of those accomplishments to not being barely able to pull one-fifth of the people that they initially helped?

I can only speculate that the GOP took the black vote for granted in the times immediately following the desegregation of America or that the Democrats wisely ripped the credit away from them. If we take a look at who was president during the most recent desegregation in the late 1960s, you had the most beautiful John F. Kennedy and then the scary, incredibly iron-fisted Lyndon B. Johnson (who was a Democrat from Texas, by the way.)

The combination of those two charismatic presidents did take some of the fuel out of the right's fire when it came to desegregation. The left had the spotlight back in the day because they had the presidency, but seriously? Was that all it took?

From there on out it was easy to spin things. And when Ronald Reagan won in 1980, the easiest thing for Democrats to do was to start saying that the GOP no longer understood black people and that they were racist. True or not, if you say something long enough, people will start to believe it. Worse yet, if you say something long enough and the people you're saying it about don't fight back against it, you'll railroad them and they'll start losing elections and arguments based on the rumors you started.

Oh, and if you doubt that it's spin that Republicans are all racist for some reason, take a look at the alternative to that. What happened with Bill Clinton ran for office? They handed the man a saxophone, put him on *The Arsenio Hall Show*, and called him the blackest president we had ever had to that point. He was even inducted into multiple African American halls of fame. Seriously? He's a white guy. A really white guy. Not too different from any of the other white guy presidents that we've had, but he is apparently qualified enough to make it into a black hall of fame. His mentor in politics was former Arkansas Senator J. William Fulbright, one of those Southern Democrats who helped filibuster and shoot down every single piece of civil rights legislation that came through the US Senate.If you don't think that's the left's ultimate successful spin on the race card, then what is?

Don't stop there though, the left went right back to accusing Republicans of being horribly racist during the George W. Bush administration. Administration? I'm sorry, let's start with the 2000 election. When Al Gore was down in the polls, Democrats started saying that Republicans didn't want black people to vote. That's it. There was no solid evidence behind that statement—they just started saying it.

From there, we had the hanging chad problem and close voting in the Miami-Dade and Broward counties in Florida, where if you turned on the news, you would frequently hear that Republicans were discriminating against the elderly Jewish and black populations of the area. Were they? Or was it just close voting? No solid evidence was ever really shown of this discrimination. It was just. Close. Voting. But, as always, the Democratic machine went to work spinning it as racist.

In 2004, to correct for all of that racism that they claimed existed, left groups turned out in droves in the major cities to ensure that there was fair and non-discriminatory voting. Where I was stationed in Philadelphia as a member of the Bush-Cheney legal team, the left had three different organizations making sure that people were given the same fair right to vote. There were up to ten different people—all of whom worked for the left—making sure there was no racial funny business going on at the polls. Ten. At that point, you go from protecting the vote of minorities to voter intimidation. All intimidation doesn't have to be violent and mean, you know. If you have ten people from one political background making sure that you get your right to vote when there is no threat around in the area that you wouldn't, you're going to be intimidated by them…bottom line.

Remember Hurricane Katrina and the quote "George Bush hates black people?" Granted, Bush made a political error by not taking a photo op picture flying over the disaster in New Orleans (which is all it would have been), but the left pounced all over the subject. Bush and FEMA failed, not because of bureaucracy, or an error, but because Republicans are racist. That was it, right? Forget just one of the many facts that George W. Bush wasn't racist, including that he named Colin Powell and Condoleezza Rice Secretary of State; he was racist because of Katrina.

The problem the entire time with the GOP is that they never made a single effort to call a duck a duck and counteract those critics head on. Even though George W. Bush did a lot for minorities to include them in his White House, the right didn't go head-to-head to combat the rumors and lies of absolute racism, and that's why they continued to lose minority votes.

The perfect storm of all the spin from the left on race came in 2008, when Barack Obama became the Democratic Party's nominee for president. To this day, if you don't agree with him, the fallback excuse is that you're a racist.

It didn't help that the fresh Barack Obama made the curmudgeonly John McCain look like the whitest, most out of touch person in America. Forget the fact that McCain had more policy and war experience than anyone else running in 2004; he was an old white man…and after all those years of spinning that Republicans didn't like black people and finally getting a black candidate for president, the Democrats had no chance of losing.

Now I just spent a few pages explaining how the left spun the Republican into racism, but I made it seem one-sided. It in-fact is not. Republicans, after not fighting back for so long, have allowed

Democrats to put an exclamation point on every single instance of potential racism that the GOP may show. A great example, as I mentioned already, is Hurricane Katrina.

For the GOP to win back black people, they need to first identify how they have been attacked for years. Knowing the devastation to minorities in New Orleans and how things could have been spun, George W. Bush should have been on the first Air Force One available to get down there, if even for the photo op. And don't you dare say photo ops are bad. Take a look at what Obama did with Chris Christie right after Hurricane Sandy and right before the 2012 polls opened. It helped him…and if Democrats pull off photo ops to show how they care and Republicans don't, conservatives leave themselves wide open for attacks and name-calling—specifically the term "racist."

This is me with Allen West, he's a member of the GOP and guess what else? He's an African-American. Some people say he's out of touch; I just say that he has a haircut from the 1980s known as the "hightop-fade."

See, we all know by now that Democrats have spun the racism card so that Republicans are weak on the subject. The right can't cough without getting a funny look from someone on the left, so why then would you allow openly racist fringe members of your party to speak at conventions and on panels? I could literally talk about this for days, but you can do your own research on it. It's happened more than a few times. Look it up. Learn how to vet people.

Alright, you convinced me; here's one story of racists not being shot down at a convention. At a convention I won't name that happened a few years ago, Scott Terry and Matthew Heimbach were in attendance at what was called the "Trump the Race Card" panel and are both pretty well known for…~~hating black people~~ really *loving* white people. They had a lot to contribute to the conversation, most of which the media took and ran with to exemplify why Republicans don't get minority votes…and I agree with the media on this one. You see, these guys were both members of the infamous White Student Union at Towson University in Maryland at that point.

Terry kicked off the horrible racist comments by saying that the GOP would function better if it were, "united like the hand, but separate like the fingers." That's right; he just jumped right into the old separate but equal comment. That didn't stir the crowd at all…. *No one was phased.* Let's continue, shall we?

Terry also went on to say that, "It seems to me that you're reaching out to voters at the expense of young white southern males like myself…" Uh-oh. It's about to get worse. For the icing on the cake, when speaking about Frederick Douglass forgiving his former master, Terry said, "Did he thank him for giving him shelter?"

The panel kind of broke down after that because Kim Brown, a friend of mine and an African American radio host, was there and had heard enough. She actually took a stand against the racist remarks from Terry that the other Republicans in the room allowed to continue, and she was basically booed by the crowd.

So in sum, what happened was that racist comments against black people were tolerated, but when a black person took a stand against them out of the crowd, she was booed. I wish I were spinning that.

My question is this: why were Terry and Heimbach even allowed to attend the conference when a simple Google search links them to a ridiculous amount of racist quotes—especially from Heimbach who has some real public zingers thanks to his having to defend the formation of the White Student Union at his college. Some of his greatest hits include:

"No longer will the homosexual, Muslim, and black supremacist groups be allowed to hijack our campus....Youth for Western Civilization is preparing to take our campus back, all we need is the help of people like you to make it happen."—Youth for Western Civilization blog, January 2012

"This is our home and our kith and kin. Borders matter, identity matters, blood matters, libertarians and their capitalism can move to Somalia if they want to live without rules, in the West we must have standards and enforce them. The 'freedom' for other races to move freely into white nations is nonexistent. Stay in your own nations, we don't want you here."—"I Hate Freedom," Traditionalist Youth Network, July 7, 2013

And...

"Those who promote miscegenation, usury, or any other forms of racial suicide should be sent to re-education centers, not tolerated."—"I Hate Freedom," Traditionalist Youth Network, July 7, 2013

I like dating women of color...so I guess I'm going to need some re-education.

It's not bad enough that the GOP already has trouble recruiting black voters to its ranks because they've been accused of being racist. They allow people like Terry and Heimbach to attend major conferences of theirs, and then practically endorse slavery without being shut up. If you weren't racist already, you're descending to it by silently watching while it happens.

If you were at a family reunion and your crazy, drunk uncle Mort got up in front of everyone and start saying racist stuff, your family would shut him up immediately and at least try to sit him down. It's just logical. People don't typically tolerate racism in America anymore. That's why when you don't shut people up at a right-wing convention, it's easy to bring legitimacy to the accusations of racism that have historically come at you from the left.

And don't get me wrong: policy and flip-flopping on issues aside, Mitt Romney wasn't a bad person to run for president, but when you play the race card, he's even whiter than John McCain—which when everything was being spun around in election time—only confounded the issues that the party was going to face against Barack Obama.

When I've spoken about racism so far in this chapter, I've only referred to African Americans. I haven't even begun to touch on the issues the GOP has with the Hispanic vote. The problem with the GOP losing Hispanic voters is that when Democrats say that they don't like them, they have a lot more evidence to back it up.

Remember how we discussed the spin that eighteen-year-olds are given to vote for Democrats? Republicans hate your gay friends and they also hate women you know, so if you are a woman or know one, odds are Republicans hate you too?

Some kids can see through that spin and logic and think clearly. It's easier to spin that "Republicans hate your family and friends" bit on the Hispanic population.

Republicans have taken a hard stand against illegal immigration. (And yes, it's called illegal immigration because there are persons from another country who have immigrated here against the law. It's a literal and not slanderous or racist term.) And why shouldn't the country take a hard stand against illegal immigration? First of all, it's just us protecting our borders from folks who want to sneak in and get benefits from living here. We have a process, albeit a long and difficult one, where aliens can become legal citizens. That's the bottom line…to a point.

According to recent polling, and I'm not sure exactly how they pull off this polling, more than twelve million illegal immigrants are living in America right now. The majority of these immigrants are of Hispanic heritage and are from a nation to the south that is not necessarily Mexico. With numbers in the millions, that means that there are more likely than not relatives of these individuals in the country already. And trust me, politicians, at least the Democrats, recognize this.

And like I said, just as they do with young voters, the left plays the password game by yelling things like, "Republicans hate (fill in a Hispanic heritage here)!" Forget the fact that the goal of the Republicans is only to follow the law and make sure that the people who the United States' free services and assistance go to are actually American citizens and immigrants who worked their butts off to legally be here in the country—Republicans hate (fill in the Hispanic heritage here) because they don't want people of that culture to illegally come into the country and reside here.

Oh, let's also not forget how *terrible* Republicans are because they want people to prove that they are who they say they are when they go to vote. That's unconstitutional! Why should someone have to prove their residency or that they are who they claim to be when they vote?! That's so disgusting…I mean, how would someone be able to illegally vote if they had to prove who they were? That would eliminate strategies including but not limited to: voting multiple times; voting under other names; voting outside of your state, including in more critical swing states; and most importantly for this chapter, voting as if you were legally a citizen of the United States and could actually vote here.

Shame on you, Republicans, for trying to keep minorities, especially Hispanic people, from voting by enacting those terrible voter ID laws where people have to prove that they are who they say they are when they vote!

Democrats are *definitely* not pandering to the Hispanic community in America by raising a stink about this! I sure hope you guys can read sarcasm or else I'm in trouble at this point.

I can't blame the left for doing it either. Why would they not want to win over the fastest growing minority group in the nation? If they could hand out checks to them (like they did with the old people) they would! But they can't, so they're manipulating and spinning while the GOP sits back and takes a hit for trying to make people follow the law.

Wait, stop right there! They are handing out checks! Has anyone ever heard of the DREAM Act? It's the dream of illegal immigrants who have children here to get discounted college for those children, so Democrats are handing out in-state college education and financial aid to them to go and get degrees!

The shocking thing is that most of my doctor and researcher friends that I mentioned at the beginning of the chapter, those minorities and persons like me who were raised in lower income demographics were fortunate to receive the moneys we did to attend college support the DREAM act. I don't because I'm logical.

My hometown hasn't changed much and there are still kids out there everywhere who are American citizens and deserve an education. These poor kids could cure cancer or AIDS or come up with cold fusion energy that could save the world, but because they aren't here illegally, their *dreams* don't matter to Democrats. Let's face it though, their votes don't really matter. If you're running the numbers and population statistics, you'd realize that the current legal population of American citizens are going to continue to basically be split down the middle for a little while, so Democrats don't care. What they do care about is a whole group of potential voters who aren't signed up to pull those levers yet.

Remember what I mentioned earlier about the Republicans who ended slavery after the Civil War? I passively mentioned something that they did that gave the old GOP wins in elections for years. Now granted, what they altruistically did to further equality in America actually did help out a group of people rather than just get votes, but it just so happened that votes continued to roll in for them for years.

Did you figure out what I'm talking about yet? They enacted the Fifteenth Amendment. Do you know what kind of power a political party has when they give freedom *and* the freedom to vote to an entire *race of people*?!

If they didn't squander their connection to these facts throughout the years by allowing spin from an opposing party to take over, they would have been in power forever!

To be exact, the GOP didn't lose the Presidency for essentially seventy-two years. Between 1860 and 1932, the Democrats were only able to elect two of their own, and those were for two terms each. Other than that, it was all Republicans all the time.

What do you think Democrats are actively trying to do here with the DREAM Act; making it villainous for police to ask illegal immigrants to show their paperwork; and villainizing voter ID laws? They've now gotten us to the point that they want to just allow those persons who came here illegally to stay here legally. Why not? Let's just jump straight over making it easier for people to become citizens and let folks who came here illegally stay legally. Let's have a pretty open border policy.

If Democrats are responsible for giving this amnesty and persons who were here illegally were suddenly allowed to vote, Democrats would control our entire political system for years to come; I'm not talking a couple of years—I'm talking the next half of a century.

So before you as a Democrat go and say that your party is just there to help out the little guy who happens to be an illegal immigrant at this point, at least acknowledge what the strategy is. And yes, some Republicans want to help back these concepts as well. That's because they basically don't have a choice. What are they going to do when millions of people who couldn't previously vote in our country suddenly become legal citizens and voters...and they, the conservatives, are found trying to defend against that? It's a really bad position to be in.

Yes, the GOP wants to uphold the law, but man, they are in a terrible position if Democrats are able to continue manipulating Hispanic immigrants and their families in America by giving handouts and rights. It's different when it's kids. Kids get older and wiser. These are rights that the government is just going to hand out to a group of people who under our current law are constitutionally here illegally.

Great strategy, Democrats. I don't have to like it and hope the Republicans can figure out how to stop it or at least turn it in their favor, and it looks like with jobs numbers they might, but for the greater part of their modern existence, the GOP has done nothing to really woo this potential gigantic voting population. It's a good thing that the Hispanic population, the same population that voted for Obama over Romney 71 to 27 percent and Hillary over Trump 65 to 29 percent, isn't going to overtake the current white population, who at least was more evenly split over Obama and Romney by size in a critical state in the next decade…. What was that? Texas? No…come on. Texas is a state that's *always* a lock for the right. It is one of the most conservative states in the union; there's no way that it could turn blue…right?

Wrong. In fact, odds are that it will turn blue just based on demographics and trends in voting, as described in "If Texas Goes Blue, Republicans Are Finished," a National Review article by George Will. It's not speculation; it's just mathematical fact. So get out your pencils and paper and put on your thinking caps to follow along. Spoiler alert: if you're a Democrat, you're about to get *really* excited. On the flipside, if you're a Republican, you're about to do the opposite of getting *really* excited.

Right now, 55.2 percent of the population of Texas is comprised of minorities, but you don't hear that from any national media outlets. Instead they make Texas look like a bunch of stupid white cowboys, right? Again, looking at the entire population of Texas, it breaks down as follows: 38.5 percent of the people in the state self-identify as Hispanic, 11.5 percent are African American and 5.5 percent are Asian American.

Keep in mind the fact in the last two elections, those three minority groups voted nationally eighty/twenty: Democrat–Republican. Ready for some of that math?

Eighty percent of 55 percent of the current population of Texas votes Democrat. That means that (and you can cheat here if you have a calculator or just play along because I'm going to give you the numbers) 44 percent of the current population of Texas votes Democrat.

That just doesn't make any sense now, does it? Because we've assumed for years now that Texas is a completely red state. Forget Lyndon B. Johnson, forget Ann Richards, and forget this little-known fact: the majority of elected officials in Texas are Democrats. Now that doesn't mean the state's House and Senate or the governor, but when you break down every single city with mayors, city councilmen, pumpkin queens, and whatever other elected municipal position that's voted for in Texas, most of those officials are Democrats.

Ready for the good news for Democrats? Over 67 percent of births in Texas, not counting immigrants or people moving in to the state, but children born in Texas in general, are from those same minority communities. That means that by the year 2040, over 80 percent of the Texas population under forty years of age will be from those groups as well.

So without any of the things that Republicans talk about fearing, like a change in immigration policy or children who are born to illegal immigrants and being granted citizenship who automatically vote Democrat upon turning eighteen…without any of that, the population grows to a point where the minority groups become even more of the majority, actually outnumbering white folks in the state. Keeping in mind that 80 percent of those groups voted for a Democrat for president, the numbers show that Texas will most likely go blue in fewer than two presidential elections with no work whatsoever by the left.

Surely the Republicans are worried about this, right?

Steve Munisteri, former chairman of the Texas Republican party from 2010 to 2015, was very open about this, and I have had many discussions about this with party leaders in the state in the past on the same topic. The number one concern about those accurate statistics is that *no one* at a national level, other than Democrats, is paying attention to them.

It's so bad that when you look at fundraising numbers—at least those that I was privy to earlier in this decade—the national Republican Party takes roughly one hundred times the amount of money in donations out of the state than what they invest into the state.

Keep in mind that Texas is worth thirty-eight Electoral College votes. If Republicans lose the state, the Democrat candidate for president could easily lock down New York, California, and Texas itself for a total of 122 votes. You only need 270 to win. That deficit would mean that the Republican nominee would need to clean up nearly every other state in the union to be elected president.

I say all that to say this: when's the last time that an elected white male Republican sat down with key African American, Asian American, and Hispanic leaders and said, "Hey, teach me." When has someone actually humbled himself or herself enough to say that they just don't get it and want to learn from people who are significantly different from them? And if they have, when's the last time that we in the public knew about it?

Listen, white people. As much as some of you conservatives out there will disagree with me, you just don't understand what minorities have gone through in this country. You don't. And the first time that you humble yourself enough to ask for a meeting with a true African American or Hispanic leader—not someone who is in it for the press and fame at this point like an Al Sharpton—but someone who is a true leader in their community, a preacher or a (dare I say it?) community organizer and say "teach me," something changes.

You will go from being that stereotype that the left has created for you—that rich white male or whatever the label is that you aren't fighting—and turn into someone who people really can't say anything bad about. You're trying to find middle ground and work with those people who you want to represent. Stop living in a bubble that has been created by the left for you and start risking it by reaching out. If you don't, we end up blue for a very long time. If you do truly act, Republicans will begin to have fighting chance to win back minority voters.

It wasn't always this way. Republicans weren't always negatively stereotyped. They didn't always get smacked in the face every time a nutcase of theirs acted out. That's because there was a time when we all kind of got along a little better and didn't get caught up in media spin.

Oh, and for God's sake, disown crazy racists. Don't let them in your conventions. And if you do, don't let them speak or wear racist clothing. If you're going to have a panel discussion at a convention with Republicans, invite minority leaders who have opposing views to discuss their issues with you, don't just wheel out the guys you have that are already on your side. If I wanted to know how awesome I was, I would buy my casual acquaintances drinks. They could blow smoke up my ass all night. If you want to truly trump the race card, how about you invite people who don't like you to come and have an open discussion as to why they don't like you? Otherwise, you'll never learn what you need to learn.

See, all I presented here was a couple of facts and numbers. And those facts and numbers typically don't bode well for Republicans. If you want minorities to vote for you again, you need to forget those stock facts about what you once did and forget the scary numbers that show that you're about to lose Texas and get to the heart of the issue by learning about the heart of people.

I know that sounded like a big liberal hippie speaking, but it's true. Stop playing that numbers game and start tackling the ugly stereotypes that the left has created for you. Once you do that, you can start winning over minorities.

This is me auditioning for Showtime at the Apollo in 2011. I didn't make it. It wasn't because I was white though; it was because I was funny to everyone in the audience except the three judges who mattered. I put this picture in here to pander to the audience and because I wrongfully believe that this picture gives me more street cred.

CHAPTER 12:

★ ★ ★

I'LL NAME THIS CHAPTER FOR YOU HALFWAY THROUGH

When I get pulled over by police officers, I get angry and I yell. I yell a lot.

I remember specifically one evening in a residential area just north of Baltimore, a police officer started following me in my newer car that I had just had freshly washed. I shifted lanes to see if he would follow me and he did. It was a reasonable time of night. I wasn't doing anything wrong and in fact, just to reinforce that, I made sure to do the speed limit to the number.

Most of us have had experiences like this. We start to think a police officer is following us, so we double check to obey the law. In this instance, I was fresh out of law school and was keen to exactly what might prompt a police officer to pull me over. He hadn't been parked so I knew that he didn't get me for speed and I remembered that my lights all worked. I was perplexed as to why this guy was literally tailing me. Then it happened. The lights and siren came on and he pulled me over.

My heart rate didn't increase because I wasn't worried that I had done something wrong; in fact, I knew that I hadn't. But as the police officer strolled up to my window, my anger began to stir inside.

I know when I speed. I have driven the country multiple times and trust me, if you catch me on the open road, I'm basically at a rate that with the right 1980s science, I would be able to travel back in time. I have only been pulled over once for speeding on a long drive and I'll never forget it because it was literally one time out of hundreds. I immediately admitted that he got me and was given a moderate fine. No big deal. This time, it was different.

The police officer came up to my window and asked me if I knew why he pulled me over. My response, and I mean this in all caps because I was yelling "I was about to ask you the same thing! Why the F-did you just pull me over?!" He was shocked. Hell, I was shocked that that came out of my mouth, but I knew that I had done nothing wrong.

He stumbled over the next sentence, "Well, uhh…I ran your plates…and uhh…your emissions test is coming up soon. I wanted to let you know."

"MY EMISSIONS TEST?! What a service! Thank you for letting me know! I hope you do this for everyone in the area." I snapped.

"You…you have a nice day, sir. You're free to go," the officer replied. He walked back to his car and drove off.

In the middle of our less-than-five-minute encounter, a group of the African American residents of the neighborhood started to form on the street. When they saw that I was a white guy, they began to yell things like "He smells like weed! Search the car!" Which, to be completely honest, is hilarious, but speaks to a much greater issue.

You see, the residential area I was driving in was a predominantly black part of a poorer neighborhood called Dundalk, just north of Baltimore. Without being able to see the driver of my slick newer looking car that was freshly washed, I was targeted by a police officer and pulled over for…drumroll please…*nothing*.

I can't speak to what the officer's intent was or why he did it, but my story seems to line up with that of many of my friends… and even a prominent Republican United States Senator.

Believe it or not, at one point I went to a gym every single day. I sure don't look it, but when I did…well, I didn't look like it either. I had a trainer there who was a former lineman who played for the University of Miami's football team. He was easily 6'3" and well over three hundred pounds—a guy who could unscrew my head with no effort with his bare hands. He was completely drug-free and kept himself in a shape that I could only hope to get to one day in my life. We became good friends, mainly because all I did was joke about how weenie I am and I was the only non-senior citizen, non-douche who went to the gym in the middle of the day. As you do with friends, you share terrible stories about stuff that happened to you.... And his were eerily similar to the one I began the chapter with.

He would make the commute back and forth from Miami to Austin frequently with his friends and would tell me that he literally hated every minute of most of the journey. "It's not an if, it's a when," he would tell me, referencing how many times he had been pulled over. He knew after the first time to not speed through certain areas, but even that didn't make a difference. On every trip, regardless his perfect driving and record, he was pulled over by police—typically in Mississippi or Alabama—and asked to exit his car. Each time he told me, an officer would berate him, push him around a bit, and make him sit on the corner and wait while they called the drug-sniffing dogs to walk around his vehicle. Every. Time.

My trainer friend doesn't look threatening, but he's a big guy. He might even be kind of known for his time on field, but he's never had a criminal record and he doesn't do drugs. He's basically as boring as me. His traveling buddies were the same: bigger guys, but literally wouldn't hurt a fly, would never touch drugs, and were always responsible people—probably more so than I. But they were pulled over consistently, pushed around and made to wait at least ten times over a two-year period on their trips back and forth from Miami to Austin.

Another friend of mine (one of the most brilliant men that I have every met) who has written policy for and advised some of the top politicians in our land has a similar experience. He, like me and basically everyone around me, is pretty boring when it comes to living on the edge with drugs and alcohol. He's completely clean, doesn't touch anything illegal, rarely gets drunk for a guy who has spent so much time in the swamp, and is incredibly responsible. He's never broken a law and he's a cautious and safe driver.

He has achieved all of his dreams in Washington, D.C. and become a great policy author and advisor, which means he comes home late from work...a lot. He has to be available to move when Congress moves, and be on top of issues as they break so that the people he advises know what has happened and how to deal with it to represent their constituencies the best that they can.

Late nights mean late drives home. Late drives home in a car that , to be completely honest, pretty pimped out. A Chrysler 300. It looked like a car a rapper would drive; I personally love how they handle, but I would never own one. I'm more of a retro hunk-of-junk guy in my older age, but I won't fault you for driving something awesome.

To get home late at night, he would have to drive through neighborhoods in urban parts of Washington, D.C. known for crime and well, not necessarily being the safest. And, while not doing anything illegal, he was pulled over a total of over thirty times. Each time, he would be questioned by the police as to what he was up to and who he was. They would sometimes pull him out of the car and make him wait for drug-sniffing dogs to come around and check to see if he was dealing. The ordeal made what was already a fourteen- to sixteen-hour day into a sixteen- to eighteen-hour day, and he was too tired to deal with it.

He couldn't take a different way home without crossing through this neighborhood, nor should he be forced to avoid it, so he did the next best thing to stop getting pulled over; he sold his car and downgraded to something less ballin'. He still gets pulled over and the same things happen to him, but now it's just a little less frequent.

He told me about this story on his own and I was shocked to learn about it. I was even more shocked when I heard his story repeated on the floor of the United States Senate and coupled with similar stories from the man talking about it.

I don't want to put words in Senator's Tim Scott's mouth, so I'll use his own from his speech

"...Over the course of one year, I've been stopped seven times by law enforcement officers. Not four. Not five. Not six, but seven times in one year as an elected official. Was I speeding sometimes? Sure. But the vast majority of the time, I was pulled over for nothing more than driving a new car in the wrong neighborhood or some other reason just as trivial."

On one occasion, Senator Scott was immediately followed by a police officer after he left a mall. He recalls making four left turns while the police officer tailed him in a car, finally being pulled over on the fourth turn, the one into his apartment complex, where the officer approached him and said that he didn't use his turn signal on *that* final turn. As if he or any of us would have failed to signal after noticing a police officer was following us or would not have obeyed every traffic law to a tee.

He also spoke of a time when he and some colleagues were going after a workout to Outback Steakhouse for food at 4 PM. He was pulled over by a police officer who informed him that he was pulling him over because he thought his car was stolen. That's right...*stolen*. Senator Scott asked the police officer if his plates were run and the car came back as a stolen car to no avail. There had been no report of Sen. Scott's car having been stolen, he had disobeyed *zero* traffic laws, and he was being pulled over and questioned as to whether or not his personal vehicle was stolen.

People are targeted, not because of doing something wrong, but because of demographics and being in an area where success or whatever you look like "seems or looks criminal." If you haven't figured it out by now, all of the people I mentioned were African-American and I am not. Honestly if you didn't know I wasn't black until now...that would be interesting to say the least.

In his own words and through his own vastly different experiences than my own, Senator Scott says "I do not know many African-American men who do not have a very similar story to tell. No matter the profession. No matter their income. No matter their disposition in life."

I guess now's the time that I should reveal to you why I labeled this chapter generically at the beginning. I wanted you to read it before I dropped the actual title on you because I didn't want your bias, especially if you're a conservative or a Republican, to make you groan, skim it, or not read it at all.

When the left talks about this topic, they yell, they stretch things too far, and they bring the conversation from the wrong place. There's nothing worse than being talked at by college kids who have no concept of the real world—those who are anti-establishment or socialists, who claim to be fighting for God-knows-what but when you argue with them, they claim that you have offended them and immediately retreat to a safe space.

You know the type: the out-of-control protestors who try to shout down the incredibly harmless Ben Shapiro in the name of fighting fascism; the type that want to have free speech and provide equality for everyone other than those who disagree with them politically. These are the people carrying the banner for what I want to talk about here, and they're the wrong people to carry the banner. They don't have the life experience, and they certainly don't have the demeanor to say what I'm about to say. In fact, they'd probably be offended and tell me that I have insulted their gender, race, sex, class, socioeconomic background, literary skills, and whatever else they can think of because of my saying that they're the wrong people to say this…but here goes:

CHAPTER 12, FOR REAL

★ ★ ★

~~I'LL NAME THIS CHAPTER FOR YOU HALFWAY THROUGH~~

WHITE PRIVILEGE IS REAL.

The entire point of sharing the stories that I did and starting by including my own is to show you that yes, there is a bias in the way that certain police deal with people of different colors.

The automatic defense to white privilege being real that comes from conservative is "Well I didn't get (insert free item) for being white. Where's my (free stuff)?" People follow that up by saying that they were poorer than most of the people they know. Trust me, I know what it was like to grow up poor and I know what it's like to watch other people get free things and handouts when I would love to have those same free things, but that's not what white privilege is about.

White privilege isn't about the good stuff that you get for being non-white; it's about the bad stuff you don't get for being white. In all my traffic stops, I have never been asked to exit my car to wait to be searched by a drug-sniffing dog. In fact, in all of my traffic stops, I have never been asked to even exit my car. On bad days or when I'm perplexed as to why I'm being pulled over, I cuss and yell at the police officers for pulling me over, just like I said in my opening story. None of the people whose stories I've mentioned here would ever think of doing what I did, and not just because they are afraid of what would happen to them, but because they are much classier than I.

The argument that white privilege exists has been dragged into the mud by so many people who can't effectively convey what it means that it's written off. You can't simply say that white privilege doesn't exist anymore because there was a black president or that black athletes and actors make millions of dollars. That argument literally makes no sense.

Yes, in America we are all equal under the law and yes, in America people of all races have an ability to do well in their given professional fields, but bad things still happen to people of color that would never happen to me based on the fact that they are people of color.

"But what if someone is discriminated against for their race?" you may say. "There are laws in place to protect them now." That is 100 percent correct, but you need to put that in perspective. Just think about what happens if people of color are discriminated against in the workplace.

If people of color are discriminated against based on their race, those who are discriminated against can now go to civil court and be given legal recourse for that discrimination, which is great, but they would have to first experience that discrimination, which would most likely involve some type of financial harm. Next, they would have to stand up against their own company or those discriminating against them, document it, and hire an attorney which may or may not cost a significant amount of money. From there, they would have to prove their case in a court of law. This entire process could take years and thousands of dollars…and is something that will not happen to me as a white person unless I apply to be a member of the cast of *Hamilton*.

Not having to experience any of that process is a privilege I have exclusively for being white.

The constant declaration that everything and everyone is racist and discriminatory when it's not, muddles the messaging of what exactly white privilege means. The left will use it to say that people on the right, and particularly white people, shouldn't have a voice when it comes to certain issues. Those college kids that I spoke of earlier will use it as a defense to out shout a conservative who is making a logical point.

The right will bring in crime statistics, which ultimately have no bearing on individual cases of discrimination. The stories I shared above were from people with no criminal record whatsoever. It pains me to see the arguments on both sides when officers shoot and kill African Americans who end up being unarmed.

From the left, we're given blanket statements that all cops are bad, white people hate anyone of color, and racism runs rampant in America. From the right, we're told to look at the criminal background of the person who was shot because clearly they did something, and we're given statistics of how black people kill the most black people.

You're both wrong.

Blanket statements about anyone are always 100 percent inaccurate. Cops and first responders are there to protect us and the first and only people who run toward the issue, not away like the rest of us (at least that's what the rest of us should be doing). Sure there are bad police officers, but they are so few and far between that it would be horrible to group them together and say they're all bad…. When one wrongfully kills someone they swore to protect, it does deserve national attention. But it should be looked at in an objective way, and not blown up to politicize that everyone is a disgusting racist. The country by and large isn't, and I cite my years of traveling and talking with real and diverse people more confidently than I do any number of hyper-polarized videos by media organizations who want to cash in on social media outrage. By the way, does anyone find it odd that some on the left will scream that not all Muslims are terrorists after an attack, but say that all cops are racist after an unarmed African American is shot?

On the right, let's cut to the chase: a past criminal record has nothing to do with a man being shot. Nothing. I don't care how terrible a person is who is accidentally shot by a police officer or shot while in police custody; unless there is a direct, proven threat to a police officer's life, there should never be shots fired. We will never know what happened in the case of Michael Brown. We do know that there were no hands in the air before he was shot, so that would be a bad topic to discuss here, but we *do know* from video what happened to Philando Castile and Alton Sterling.

At no point was Philando Castile a threat to the police officer who shot him. The police officer was afraid and fired on him incorrectly, tragically taking his life.

And in the case of Alton Sterling, the video clearly shows the man lying on the ground, and although he was struggling, he was in an impossible position to pull a weapon to even remotely injure the officer on top of him. So when the officer rolled off of him and literally unloaded his gun on the man, killing him, something was terribly wrong.

In either instance, it doesn't matter if these two men were the worst criminals in the history of America. Castile made no sudden movements and posed no threat to the police officer, and Sterling could have been taken down with a punch to the back of the head if things were *that* bad. Both men would—and *should*—be alive today but for the incorrect actions of the officers involved, regardless of any criminal activity in the past.

Ultimately, the problem with the white privilege issue is that the far left, especially on college campuses, screams about it so much in the wrong instances that it has ultimately tainted the term for everyone. It's used to shout down a white person or conservative with whom leftists disagree and it's used to cover for failings of individuals who find it easier blame others and to scream a term rather than take personal responsibility for their actions.

The problem is this: even though the term is legitimate, and it has been proven over and over again that people of color are treated more negatively and put in positions that white people will never understand, the overuse of the term by the far left has ruined the concept and kept many on the right from listening to its basic meaning because almost every single context that it's used in is exaggeration to escape reasonable debate.

Where solutions could be made to help everyone if both sides came together, incorrect semantics by the ridiculous have kept us apart.

CHAPTER 13:

★ ★ ★

SO YOU'RE TELLING ME THAT YOU MADE AN INFORMED DECISION? YOU'RE SO ADORABLE!

How do you vote in an election? And you better have not have said that you go to a polling place and pull a lever or punch a chad or touch a screen—you get the point as to how you shouldn't have answered.

Do you really look at all the issues in an election? Do you look at candidate's history or experience? Do you vote blindly for your team? Or are you merely voting for the best-looking person?

I bet you think you're smart enough to lie and convince yourself that you actually looked at all the issues and did your research, but I bet you didn't. I'm willing to bet that you didn't take the hours of time to painstakingly review every piece of each candidate's platform in order to make an informed decision, but rather watched a lot of TV and read a lot of op-eds in your favorite publications to make your decision.

And there's no harm in doing that if you enjoy living in a world where people who don't really care about you hand everything to you on a platter. I mean, I care about you too; that's why I wrote this book and handed it to you on a shelf or through the internet like I was giving you the warming hug of snarky knowledge, right?

All kidding aside, everything that we receive through the media is biased. *Everything.* So when we draw lines in the sand and say one organization is more biased than another and they're disgusting for it, what we're really saying is. "I don't agree with that organization's opinion."

This is nothing new. In fact, the only thing that is new is this modern concept of "fair and balanced" news coverage. Years ago, this never existed. In fact, newspapers were known to be in the pockets of political parties and the message was largely clear propaganda. Then, magically, out of the blue one day at a sales meeting or executive meeting (you can imagine the boardroom as smoky and *Mad Men*-esque as you'd like it to be here) some old curmudgeon or young bright mind (again, play to your imagination) stood up and said, "I've got it! What if we brand ourselves differently and say we take no sides? Then *everyone will buy our paper!*"

The entire boardroom was stunned into thought-provoked silence and unanimously said, "You've struck gold, Johnson!" All old-timey business scenarios involve some guy named Johnson, just to let you know.

And guess what? Their plan worked!

Want to know how I know it worked? It doesn't take a rocket scientist to figure it out. The dialogue evolved with the business. Each organization slowly evolved from openly being in the corner of a certain candidate to pretending that they didn't openly support any candidate. Then the national conversation evolved to keep up. We Americans went from knowing who was biased to pretending to not realize they were biased and pointing fingers and yelling anytime someone slipped up from the grand charade.

Are you above being a part of that charade? Nope. In fact, any time that you mention a news network, you know which way this unbiased organization leans. The obvious cable news network that has been under fire is Fox, obviously, because they are one of roughly two right-leaning cable networks. The rest lean left. All of them. It's that easy. I was going to list them all out for you here, but I figured it was easier to mention Fox News and group all the others together.

But why is Fox so gleamingly right? After all, they actually do show the opposing views a lot, and in a fair and balanced manner. It's because every other network in competition with Fox thinks that it's a good idea to yell "righty," at them all day long. This accomplishes only one thing: it makes Fox the number one news network in the country because it tells people where to go.

"Hey, you're on the right? Go watch Fox. Hey, you hate the right? Well then go watch Fox as well and be angry at their political commentary."

It's that simple.

Robots don't write the news, unless of course you count people with no personalities as robots—and I've met a lot of those in my career. In that case, robots *do* write the news. Sadly, I dated a few of those very successful, yet horribly boring women. God bless them; they're so good at their jobs, but don't expect them to know anything outside of what they write about. I say all of that to say this: every human being has an opinion, and that comes out in their work in one way or another. Also, I've dated some terribly boring reporters.

Case in point: the National Press Club's decorations. The completely non-biased home of the non-biased press covers its walls in photos of past guests and dignitaries who have attended events. I don't know that many of you will have the pleasure of walking the grandparent's house/moth ball perfumed hallways of the club in your lifetime, but if you do, you'll quickly realize that the walls are covered with pictures of everyone's favorite Democratic elected officials. There's William Jefferson Clinton and Lyndon Baines Johnson and Ted Kennedy and William Jefferson Clinton and William Jefferson Clinton. Did I mention that Bill Clinton is *all over the place*? But the media isn't biased.

Fact: at one point I hung my picture on the wall there, and it took over two weeks and a Facebook post showing the photo for them to realize I had done so. My headshot fit right in with all the stodgy old people on the wall.

Now that we've established that news organizations are run by human beings who have opinions, we need to ask ourselves why they are in existence: money.

They exist to make money, people. They aren't around to altruistically inform the public. That would be boring and no one would want to read or watch it. This isn't something that they don't know. That's why you have opinion sections and that's why you have races to break the news. That's also where the term "new media," comes from.

I'm the median line of the understanding what new media is. For the most part, if you're older than me, you'll use the term new media to describe the digital age and everything people my age and younger (rapscallions as some elders choose to call us) do on the internet. To the rest of us, new media is just, well, media.

New media is a means for those old journalists to shake a cane and separate themselves from their successors. See, they aren't too happy that news has gone from twenty-five-hundred-word tome-style articles discussing all the details of the story that you both want and don't ever need to hear to tweets of two hundred eighty characters or fewer telling you the exact same thing without all the big words and filler. They also aren't thrilled that because of the digital age that their ability to find informants and get a scoop have been ripped out from beneath them. Odds are in today's world that the whistleblower will have tweeted about the news—and been retweeted by a younger, less experienced journalist—while that older guy is still waiting for a call on his rotary phone (in a smoky office again, because that's how everything once functioned in society). The elders' only joy now comes from calling the new, more successful journalists "new media," and laughing when a news organization misfires while trying to strike first.

A great example of this was when the decision for Obamacare came out. I was actually assigned to listen to the arguments in the Supreme Court for a news organization and knew, just knew, that someone was going to screw something up. It was the perfect storm for it to happen.

You see, the Supreme Court operates under old school rules. No technology whatsoever is allowed in the court room when it's in session. It makes no sense, but those are the antiquated rules. Everything has to be stored down the steps out of the gallery where you are seated and down a lengthy hallway in the media office. All you can take into the courtroom are pens, paper, and the power of your mind. Oh, and one other thing: once you leave the press gallery, you can't get back in. You either stay and get all the information, or you leave and get locked out.

Obamacare was a big deal case. How big of a deal? I had been reporting in the Supreme Court for a few months and generally, media could stretch out and take a nap in the gallery because for the most part, no media organization cares about 90 percent of the rulings. These directly affect minor laws that then trickle down to shift minor aspects of our rights. Obamacare was different for many reasons, but in this case, the media orgs decided it would be best to "bring in the big guns." The blonde babes you see on TV, the good-looking people that are the faces of the organizations were all there, lined up and ready to report on legal issues and terms that they probably had trouble spelling merely because it was the place to be.

I wasn't there for the ruling on Obamacare, but I can tell you exactly what happened. CNN wanted to break the story first so they could win the new media game, and they did. Their blonde started to hear the decision and excused herself early; she had this locked down! She ran down those steps, having probably packed light that day so she didn't have to check out of the media room, and ran directly out the front of the Supreme Court building—like the reverse of Rocky's glorious run through Philadelphia, but in heels—to her awaiting cameraman with a live feed, and the rest was history.

Even some Congressmen listened to the report and celebrated the end of Obamacare.

Shame on them, but hey, they got there first or something.

This type of reporting and the shift to breaking news evolved from everything that I've spoken about here. American likes to be voyeuristic. We want to know everything about everyone in power. And we want that information right now! It's the reason that we don't have that much positive news to report. The idea of the voyeur is that you're seeing something that you're not supposed to see: violence, scandals, previously private things. That's what sells, so that's what they're going to spin for you.

The catalyst for the reaction that is this new media came in the first-ever televised presidential debate between John F. Kennedy and Richard Nixon. History recalls that two different winners were declared in this debate. Nixon won if you were listening to his words and policy (the actual stuff you should be voting for) over the radio. Kennedy dominated though if you watched on TV. Why? Because Nixon was sick and sweaty during the debate. He literally wasn't as attractive as Kennedy was. That's why he lost that debate. And in that extraordinarily superficial moment, media would never be the same again.

The real debate is whether or not it's the media or our own faults. I can blame either because I wasn't alive then, but people wanted to see more attractive public officials and they judged on that appearance. The media knew they would buy into the looks and started stretching more. When they confirmed that looks counted in politics as much as they did in Hollywood, they knew they could start to entertain people in similar ways.

From that point on, we were given even more spin. People cared more about the First Lady and what she did, they cared about what clothes people wore, and they cared if someone was cool or not. John F. Kennedy was unfortunately assassinated, but it would have been interesting to see how history would have handled that "sexy and cool" president's terribly failing policies had he had to stand and answer for them down the road. Instead, we see him canonized like popular artists who left this earth too soon when he really only had just a few good lines.

We saw something similar with President Obama. Obama got away with murder...literally. He chose who he could pick off with drones, he tried to start a war, he broke nearly one hundred promises, and he was setting us up to believe that the economy had no hope of recovery to the levels it's reached now. The list goes on and on, but you know what? He was a really cool guy.

Forget all the failures; Obama is fun and hip. Need I say more? The media found their way to spin things and that's what they fed us. They cheered him when he arrived, they rarely if ever challenged him, and when he left, they cried. They literally cried. It's pathetic when you think about it.

So when you go to vote at the polls, you're not listening to Richard Nixon on the radio and hearing the actual words coming out of the candidates' mouths. ou're being given seven-layer opinion dip in sexy packaging.

The media's spin on politics is remarkably similar to Jamie Oliver's exposure of American foods. You might remember what he did with this a few years ago.

He loved exposing that rather than eating quality chicken meat from a chicken or actual beef from a cow, we're fed processed leftovers and waste trimmings from both chicken and beef that get ground down, treated with ammonia, and turned into essentially the evil pink slime that ran under the city in Ghostbusters 2. That slime can then be fried and cooked into whatever delicious processed burger or chicken nugget that a restaurant wants to sell you, packaged brightly and presented with toys for your kids to eat. It's no longer good enough to hear what someone has to say and hold them accountable for it; it needs to be chopped up, presented with bright red, white and blue colors with an incredible video package and music running in the background, all the while being read to us by gorgeous people.

That my friends, is how many of our votes are influenced.

P.T. Barnum is credited with the phrase, "There's a sucker born every minute." And he ran circuses. I bet he'd be great at producing news.

So what can we do about the media? Nothing.

Are you going to call all your friends so they can write to your local news station so that your letters can be ignored? Are you going to stop watching networks you don't agree with?

I always said that if we stopped buying gas all at once for a week, the prices would drop well below two dollars, but who am I fooling? America doesn't have the ability to pull together and boycott something all at once. Sorry to disappoint you.

Every other week since Trump was elected, there has been a call for a boycott of something because of politics and it never does anything more than create a relatively trending hashtag on Twitter for a few hours. I'm looking directly at you, people who "boycotted the NFL" after players were allowed to take knees then posted *the very next week* how you were upset at how certain football players didn't perform well enough to get you a win for your fantasy team.

The only way that you can overcome the bias and become an informed voter is to make your own decisions. You don't have to sit back and take what's handed to you as fact. You can watch speeches, read candidate websites directly to see how they represent themselves, then look at multiple sources, both foreign and domestic, to research candidates on your own.

Warning: this process will take hours and hours and might actually involve you learning a little bit more about our country's history. It's going to be like giving up on your favorite fast food place and eating broccoli for a week. It ain't flashy, but it's good for you. And once you're on that path, you'll want to help others. The good thing is that there are only a few hundred million more people who can vote that we need to convince to do the same. Sounds completely unreasonable.

★ ★ ★

CHAPTER 14

THE PROBLEM IS PERSONAL RESPONSIBILITY

I woke up one morning when I was twenty-three years old and realized that I was fat. How fat? Very fat. I was 5'10" like I am now, but I weighed nearly three hundred twenty pounds. I wore a size 19-19.5 inch neck shirt and size 48 jeans. My t-shirts were 2 XL and fit me if I stretched them to be comfortable in or 3 XL if I wanted them to fit. My suit jackets were a size 54.

I specifically remember one trip to Macy's where I asked if they had my size suit in stock to buy. I had just started a new internship and wanted to have something nice to wear. The shocking response was, "I'm sorry, we don't carry sizes that big." I'll never forget that day and that feeling. I was too big for the store. They literally didn't carry anything that would fit me.

From that point forward, I decided that I would be "body positive." I was proud of being such a large person. In fact, I wanted to eat more and force everyone to respect

me for the size that I chose to be. After all, it wasn't my fault that I was fat or that I felt bad about being fat, it was society's. My parents fed me inappropriately and advertisements made food look delicious. If someone made fun of me for my size, I told them that they were just jealous fat-shamers and I retreated to my apartment to blog about it and get as much support from the internet that I could get. As far as Macy's goes, I started an online petition to end their discrimination against my size. They needed to be more inclusive and change what they stocked on their shelves to fit all people and I wanted them to know that…wait a second…No…I didn't do any of that. I did the opposite.

I realized that I had a problem. Being overweight and morbidly obese at times was a bit genetic on my mother's side of the family. On my father's side, everyone had high blood pressure. I was a walking health time bomb and it was only a matter of time that I, as a three hundred twenty pound twenty-three-year-old, was going to have a heart attack. I wasn't "body positive," in fact, I would call myself body negative. I hated how I felt. I hated that I had to wake up every morning and squeeze into my clothes, and I sat devastated in my car after that trip to Macy's wondering how I had gotten to that point.

If I continued to live the way I did, I was in trouble. So literally that day, I looked in the mirror one last time and took the last trip to fast food that I ever would in my life. I went straight to Taco Bell and I ordered a Nachos Bell Grande with a burrito and two tacos and told myself that was it…and it was.

After Taco Bell, I did some research on great ways to lose weight. After a few hours of research that night, I determined that I would cut out fast food, soda, alcohol, sugars, and dairy products altogether. I increased my protein intake and began to go to the gym every day. On the days that I didn't go to the gym, I went for long walks, jogged what little I could, and did pushups or sit-ups at home. After three years of this strict diet and exercise, not a day more or less, I finally weighed less than two hundred pounds, forty-three pounds less than I did in eighth grade. Yes, I was a fat kid too…husky-sized.

Dieting sucks. Working out sucks. Nothing is fun about cutting back and working hard to get yourself healthy. The worst part? It's a complete lifestyle change…. There's no going back to eating unhealthy unless you want to go through that pain and diet again and again.

Nearly a decade after I lost the weight, I made the correct mistake of buying twenty-eight pounds of Robin Eggs Easter Candy the day after Easter. Why would I do this? Because I'm an adult, I get to do adult things, and Robin Eggs are God's gift to the world. I ate every last one of those suckers before Christmas. That's right. Between April and December, I consumed twenty-eight pounds of the best Easter candy that has ever been and ever will be created… and I gained thirty-six pounds in those seven months.

When the final bag of Robin Eggs was being consumed, I knew that I was having problems. My jackets weren't fitting and I was feeling sluggish. I had stopped stepping on a scale a few months before because I broke the two hundred five pound plane of existence and I knew I was headed toward what I called, "critical mass." I was in trouble with my weight. So I sued the Whoppers company for creating such a delicious candy in order to rectify the damage they caused me…Wait…no. I didn't. I went back on that horrible diet that I lost over one hundred twenty pounds on years before and lost forty pounds—a few extra for good measure—before my birthday in August.

To this day, I have to watch what I eat and work out regularly or else I gain weight quickly. That is my responsibility, not anyone else's. I have to look out for my own health and wellbeing and force myself to maintain it or else I know exactly the negative results that will occur.

My actions cause results that I am responsible for. This seems like a very simple concept, but it's not. I can't blame anyone else for making me live an unhealthy lifestyle.

Loosely speaking, there's an eighteen-step process that one goes through in order to put food in your mouth as an adult and I want to break it down for you.

1. You decide what you want to eat.

2. You determine which store you would like to go to to purchase this food.

3. You walk out your front door to the mode of transportation that you will take to get to the location to purchase this food.

4. You enter the store.

5. You walk to the area of the store where you then;

6. You select which brand of food you would like to purchase.

7. You walk that food to the counter to pay for it.

8. You hand the food to the cashier who then rings you up.

9. You pull money or a credit card out of your pocket to purchase the food.

10. You take the food to your mode of transportation to go home.

11. You travel home.

12. You unpack the food from the bag it is in.

13. You open the packaging that the food.

14. You heat up or prepare the food if it needs to be prepared.

15. You move the prepared food to the place where you will consume it.

16. You put the food in your mouth.

17. You chew the food.

18. You swallow the food.

Now that process is a little shorter for people who are just going to fast food or a restaurant to eat, but you get the point. There are roughly eighteen steps between thinking about eating a certain food and putting the food in you. That's a lot of effort and commitment to live an unhealthy lifestyle if you think about it, ut at which of those eighteen steps is someone other than yourself forcing you to keep going? None.

At any of those points, and there probably could be many more, you can stop yourself from putting food in your mouth and change your lifestyle...but many don't. Don't get me wrong; I'm not bringing up all of these steps to condemn you for being who you are. I'm bringing up all of these steps to condemn you and those people who then find a way to blame someone else for their body weight.

If you don't feel good about yourself, it's up to you to change that; it's not the world's job to meet you where you are. That's what body positivity is all about: blaming someone else for your body issues.

Every single day people struggle with weight, weight loss and staying healthy...and it's not easy to do, but they do it because they are taking personal responsibility. The concept of *you* having to accept *me* for who I am or "body positivity" is lazy and pawns off the feelings of negativity you have about yourself on the world.

It's not my job to make you feel good that you made bad decisions and don't feel good about them.

I read an article recently in *Cosmopolitan* where a morbidly obese "model" went to Times Square in a bikini and expected negative comments about her body. The article and stunt were staged because she knew that if she walked out into the bustling center of the world and dropped her clothes, that people would ogle her and say something negative about her...because she herself ultimately knows she doesn't look good.

Instead of getting heckled for being incredibly out of shape and not pleasant on the eyes in a bikini, her stunt went awry. Men began to catcall her, telling her that she was a "sexy BBW" and asking her to do things like twerk. She was equally as offended. How dare these men catcall a morbidly obese woman in a bikini who dropped her clothes in Times Square for attention? Surely, it was their fault for hurting her feelings that she initially assumed would be hurt because she staged a spectacle of her overweight body that she knew most of the world would think is disgusting to look at. How dare they threaten her stable "body positivity" by yelling at her?

As I struggled to read through the article and look at the pictures, it became extraordinarily clear to me that this woman took literally zero personal responsibility for her actions. It was never her fault that she was unhealthy and large. It was never her fault that she decided to pose as nude as she could possibly be in Times Square. She was definitely not there for attention and to be outraged. And even though she was catcalled for being sexy instead of being mocked for being morbidly obese and unattractive in Times Square, it was never her fault for finding a way to be outraged even though it stood against her initial hypothesis of outrage from her actions.

Anyone with common sense would agree that even if we gave her being okay with being overweight, it was her free will and choice to place herself in the middle of New York City in a bikini knowing full well what could and most likely would happen. Why did the world have to change for just her when it was her actions that caused the issues?

This is the problem that I have with most of modern progressive policy. It's *never* the individual's fault. Don't get me wrong here: there are a lot of bad scenarios that people can find themselves in that they can't control, but for the piles of scenarios they bring on themselves, it's not the world's job to meet them where they are. You can't just declare yourself a victim after you put yourself in your scenario.

It's not just a weight issue either. It's any issue that people choose to flaunt in someone's face to force them to accept. Let's pick a fun one out of the air, shall we?

Cyber bullying.

If you're a victim of cyber bullying as an adult, it's pretty much your own fault. As a child, you could argue that you aren't trained in how the world works…but as an adult, you literally have no excuse for allowing yourself to be cyber bullied. This is just another instance, similar to the obese woman in the bikini in Times Square, of "what did you think was going to happen?"

Every single day that I send a tweet out from my Twitter on the internet or my phone, I get negative reactions. It doesn't matter the time of day or the content in the tweet or the gif that might be attached; there is always someone who is going to say something negative about it. I typically get something like "Political comedian? You aren't funny," which, at this point in the book, you might agree with. Sometimes we get even more creative or nasty and once a week, someone will typically go through more than ten tweets of mine and troll each one. Occasionally I read the comment and move on, but most of the time, I don't pay attention.

In this instance, I could claim that people are cyberbullying me. They tell me I'm not good at my job, they get nasty about my family, friends, hair, appearance, and so forth. I really have a case for playing the victim card, but I don't because I'm an adult.

If I don't like someone, the internet provides many means by which you can rid yourself of them. From blocking to muting on Twitter, to blocking and muting on Facebook and blocking and sending to spam on email, there are options. Surely people are aware of these tactics to prevent themselves from being cyber bullied…right?

Let's take this a step further: say you write articles for certain websites and those websites rely on comments from their readers for traction on their page. Speaking from personal experience, almost every single article that I have ever authored has had some type of negative comment on it…no matter how incredible that article is. When I read these comments, I don't cower in fear and fall into the fetal position crying to myself that I've been bullied; I ignore them as internet fodder and carry on with my life. It's not hard to avoid.

Say you don't know how to avoid cyberbullying by all the means that I mentioned above. What then can you do?

A simple strategy that I've found is that you simply don't read the comments and replies to your online posting. I know that's crazy, but one of the best ways to avoid making yourself a victim of cyberbullying, is to, not read the comments. An insane concept to some of you I'm sure, but it's an option to allow you to not be a victim. YouTube even has an option to turn off comments and likes or dislikes on videos. I know—crazy, right? So that you can avoid seeing the negative things that would make you believe that you were cyber bullied.

There's one ultimate way to avoid cyberbullying as an adult, and I know this is going to sound incredibly crazy to you. Turn your computer and phone off and go outside. You see, the concept of cyberbullying is that you're online and participating. You can't be cyber bullied if you aren't there to be bullied…but you really can't be cyber bullied at all.

The following are all optional activities for you: going online, reading posts, posting, participating in forums, and last but not least, not walking away from negativity.

In order to be cyber bullied, you have to be a willing participant in your own bullying. You, for the most part as an adult, are personally responsible for your behavior and what you take offense to online. You don't have to be there, but you put yourself there voluntarily and stay there to be cyber bullied. This willing neglect of self-awareness and lack of personal responsibility is one of the core differences between the thought processes of people arguing politics every single day and it brings me back to the first story I told you about the obese woman in the bikini.

It wasn't just that she was lacking in personal responsibility and pretending that she didn't put herself in the position she was in to be harassed; it was that she was looking to be offended. One of the major issues in the world today is that people aren't being offended by other's actions—they are literally taking offense.

One of my comedy advisors once told me to take risks on stage and clarified by saying "You don't offend people; people take offense." Breaking down that statement and putting it into terms of personal responsibility makes all the difference in our modern world.

Think about what happens on college campuses when students lose their minds at Ben Shapiro events. I bring up Ben Shapiro because I think he's one of the kindest, least offensive people in the world. He's a smart guy who has made one hell of a living by touring and giving lectures on conservatism. Unlike his former counterpart, Milo Yiannopolos, Shapiro doesn't lower himself to pull off stunts and be shocking. He merely shares his thoughts in an intelligent and informed way. Also, I like him because he retweets me. That all aside, I'm unsure as to how anybody or anyone could be offended by his words or actions, but they are—or at least they claim to be.

When Shapiro tours on campus, he speaks to packed audiences of hundreds at a time, giving them essentially lectures on modern conservative opinion. Almost inevitably, there are protestors who yell and challenge him, claiming that what he is saying is hateful and offensive to them. Think about this logically and similarly to cyberbullying; if you knew you were going to be offended and outraged by someone, why would you put yourself in a position to listen to them for ninety minutes? The answer is simple: you're not being offended at all. Instead, you are taking offense.

Taking offense is actively seeking out something to be offended by. If an African American is walking down the street and is called a racial slur, they are offended. They've done nothing proactive to seek out that offense to bring it upon themselves, and they don't deserve it. Conversely, if someone shows up to a comedy show where they know any topic can be discussed and the comedian drops a joke about rape or sex—whether or not it's in good taste—and someone is outraged about it, they have proactively taken offense.

Think about the outrage over MAGA hats. While I was writing this book, a teenager was assaulted by an adult man in a Whataburger in Texas because he was wearing the hat. As is usual, the Twittersphere erupted with commentary on both sides of this issue, but what was atypical at the time were outcries, especially from celebrities about the hat itself.

The Make America Great Again hat is simply a slogan on a cheap red cap like the one Donald Trump wore during his 2016 campaign. The original more than likely was printed at a Lids in under an hour just to give Trump something to wear at an event. People who supported the now-president ate them up and by now typically own one (if you don't, you're not an OG fan). After the boy was assaulted, many opponents to Trump said that this hat was offensive to them because they saw it as a symbol of racism, hate, misogyny, islamophobia, and the like. The list goes on and on.

Is the MAGA hat actually offensive? The answer to that is simple: no. It's just a cheesy hat. So why are so many people outraged about it? Because they have proactively chosen to take offense.

I could easily take offense to any baseball team's slogan that isn't "Let's Go, Mets!" After all, I think other teams are hateful for beating my favorite team, the New York Mets, repeatedly and easily throughout the years, but I don't. Why? Because the words are just words on a shirt. People voluntarily wear these slogans and chant things not to offend me, but to cheer on the team that they have come to know and love. The same is true in politics.

People aren't wearing MAGA hats to offend others; they're wearing them to show that they supported President Trump. They aren't even remotely wearing them to say they hate someone else and certainly that teenager wasn't wearing that hat to pick a fight with an adult male who was double his size and nearly double his age. Those who are offended are creating that offense in their own heads and by their own standards and refuse to take personal responsibility for this offense.

If you're one of these people who take offense to a simple red hat with a campaign slogan on it, that's your own damn fault. You've constructed a story about it being offensive to you in your own mind and you have reacted to that story. If you feel the need to assault someone because of something that you pro-actively took offense to, that is also your own fault. This shouldn't have to be explained, but it seems that in the world in which we exist, fewer and fewer people understand this anymore.

You're in this world alone and it's your personal issue. It's not the world's job to come to you and make you feel better. It's your job to correct for your issues.

It is your fault if you are catcalled or mocked if you're an obese woman who is wearing a bikini in public to put on a spectacle of yourself. It is your fault if you log online to participate in forums and on platforms where cyberbullying can occur, are cyber bullied, and then do nothing to change the scenario in which you voluntarily participate. And it is your fault if you take offense to something that someone wears or says when it isn't directed at you or is a general statement.

It was my fault that I allowed myself to get to three hundred twenty pounds and a size where there were no clothes that fit me in a Macy's. But instead of forcing everyone in the world to bow to me; instead of making excuses for the terrible physical condition that I was in; and instead of taking offense to the world appreciating healthier people, I took action and personal responsibility to change myself.

It's much easier to blame other people and use your words to condemn everyone around you than to stand up and admit that you're wrong. It's certainly much easier to tell people that they need to be more "body positive" than identifying that the only reason you use that term is to cover for your own body negativity. And it's much easier to sit on your ass and be rewarded with social media likes and retweets because you have created your own victimhood.

Personal responsibility is at the core of so many of the issues, policies, and debate that we deal with today. Should Americans have to take a stand for ourselves, or should we put it in the hands of the government and law enforcement to protect us from things that we can protect ourselves from?

That's an issue affecting both parties. Where do you draw the line? And when the government gets involved to regulate and protect things, what do we give up for that regulation and protection?

It ain't pretty—neither would I have been in a speedo at three hundred twenty pounds(or now for that matter)—and I say that while looking directly at you, obese woman in a bikini that made a spectacle of yourself. It's not the world's fault that you do what you do. It's your own.

CHAPTER 15:

★ ★ ★

ON CIVILITY

I like that I titled this chapter of the book "On Civility," because when you speak about being civil with one another or just being nice to one another, you're required to make it sound like you're an NPR show speaking above the heads of the commoners with your nose in the air and a slight British accent. The term civility itself has been taken over by people on the left that want to sound like they are above the rest of you because they are the moral superior.

The concept of civility is a simple one: don't be an asshole to people with whom you disagree. You can be mean and raise your voice in a debate, but don't go doing dumb shit to actually harass someone and make them feel unsafe because you disagree with them. And I can't believe that I'm going to have to *also* explain what unsafe means, because at the same time they raise their uppity British accents to speak about civility, the left also screams about not feeling safe. To tell you the truth, a lot of them have never actually felt unsafe in their lives and use it as an excuse to hide when they don't want to debate.

So why are we even discussing civility? How did this term get added to our lexicon over the past two years? And who is being uncivil?

The basic concept of civility, which I mentioned above, the whole not being an asshole thing, isn't why this concept has been raised in the Trump era. In fact, it's pretty far from it. You see, in the middle of campaigning for president, it was becoming obvious that Donald Trump was appealing to flyover country, the south, and, well, basically anywhere that wasn't a liberal metropolitan bubble. The liberal metropolitan bubbles were all Hillary Clinton, and a lot of the people that vote there believe the same way that Hillary does about flyover country. Shall we review those beliefs?

Flyover country and the south to them are places full of dirty, uneducated rednecks. They are the uncles that want to talk politics at holiday dinners but are "too stupid" to hold a candle to anything that you, as bubble dwellers, think and know about the world. People who don't live in the bubble shop at places like Walmart, they watch NASCAR, and they don't have all their teeth. They probably drive pickup trucks, wear a lot of camouflage, hunt and fish for fun, and worst of all, go to Christian church on Sundays.

Going to church is the worst thing in the world to a bubble dweller. How stupid are you that you believe in the Bible and that Jesus healed people and that praying to him can actually help improve your life? The bottom of the absolute barrel would be of course if you believe that God created the world in seven days. NPR commentators would call you a young-earth creationist and even though it's you believing in your Christian religious doctrine, you're viewed as an idiot for doing so. How dare you? You deplorables that don't understand how the civil world lives…. You poor, out of touch uncivil beings. You disgust them.

That is where the term civility comes from in our political spectrum today. It's a labeling of status. If you live in areas that didn't vote for Hillary Clinton or you voted for Donald Trump, you are labeled uncivil, and when you're being told that we need to be more civil, it has nothing to do with not being an asshole; it has *everything* to do with not being a metropolitan bubble-dweller who views the world only through their progressive-colored glasses.

If it were actually about being civil, many aspects of the Women's March would have legitimately upset people on the left. First, women who were pro-life were told that they were not welcome to march with the masses in the Women's march. They were considered second class citizens because of their belief that it's more than a fetus in a woman's womb when she's pregnant. Again, this is a call-back to Christian values and beliefs. Many of those who are pro-life are religious, and that isn't considered civil. If they were actually trying to be civil at that march, they would have been inclusive of *all women,* regardless their beliefs on certain issues. After all, they were all there to stand against Donald Trump; why wouldn't you want people who lean conservative issues to walk arm and arm with you? Oh, that's right, you don't consider them civil.

The next glaring thing that one could noticed at the women's march were the signs. Most of them said *super-duper* civil things like "Fuck Trump." That seems like something a totally reasonable and civil human being would say in a totally reasonable and civil conversation about the newly elected president of the United ed States, right? As I said earlier, there were also tons of women dressed up as very graphic vaginas, which again seems like something a totally reasonable human being in a totally civil conversation would do. Then there were the bloody tampon puppets, the disgustingly sexual drawings of Trump, and lots of messages about him having a small penis. Again, this seems totally reasonable and civil for a normal human being to have.

Then there were the speeches on stage. There were totally civil people doing totally civil things like ask for the White House to be blown up, or talk in graphic detail about how their menstrual blood runs down their legs. They also screamed "Fuck Trump" and yelled about how there will be registries and no rights remaining once the current president took office. Nothing to see here—these are the actions of totally reasonable people. They definitely weren't trying to cause a panic or create paranoia based on no facts whatsoever; they're just civil people doing normal human civil things.

And they consider what they're doing to be civil because they think that everyone else who isn't them is an uneducated, uncivil mouth-breather. Period.

The concept of civility isn't one of not being assholes to one another; it's just a classy sounding uppity way for actual assholes to label people that they consider to be "white trash."

"We need to be more civil with one another" is just someone saying you need to be more like me, you piece of trash human that voted for Donald Trump and can't carry on educated conversation the way that I can.

The problem with this concept of civility is that now that progressives in the bubble have labeled themselves as such to justify their actions, they believe that they can do literally anything to you, the uncivil, because what they're doing is ultimately fine and above board.

About a year ago, I was at a crappy Mexican restaurant on Capitol Hill with a good friend of mine. As you do on the Hill, you drink a lot, crush nachos when able, and pretend that you're there to discuss more things than just what happened in the news and politics that day.

In the middle of our conversation, she pointed out that Kathleen Sebelius, former Secretary of Health and Human Services under Obama, was sitting two tables away. You might remember her from the failed Obamacare rollout a few years ago. Things didn't go really well when she was in office to the point that Jon Stewart even tore her to shreds on *The Daily Show* for her failures.

"You sure that's her?" I said to my friend who can identify anyone in politics in DC because that's her job.

"Oh yeah, I think she lives around here," she replied.

We finished rambling about politics and polished off a pitcher of margaritas a few minutes later and were ready to leave the restaurant. I looked up from the ridiculously expensive check (it's the Hill) and realized that not only was Sebelius still eating her dinner, but that I would be passing by her table on the way out of the place. What happened next will shock you.

When we were walking out of the restaurant, the former Secretary's eyes and mine met and I smiled and nodded at her. She did the same. The end.

I don't agree with many of the things that Sebelius was working on under Obama and I definitely think that her work on Obamacare hurt many Americans then and continues to hurt many Americans today, but she was eating dinner and neither one of us were on what I have called "the playing field" for it to even make sense to discuss politics with one another. That's what civility looks like.

My friend and I saw someone who we could possibly argue politics with professionally, but instead of getting in her face, interrupting her meal and yelling about our differences, we acknowledged each other cordially and continued about our private lives.

Such cannot be said about a recent trend in "civility" from those who use the term to divide us into classes. The Secretary of Homeland Security, Kirstjen Nielsen, found herself eating a *much classier* Mexican restaurant in D.C. and faced a much different fate then what happened with my interaction with Sebelius.

First I want to mention, and not by name, that the Mexican restaurant Nielsen was eating at is expensive garbage. I've been there a few times for happy hour and I felt completely unfulfilled by the food and drinks I had at the place. I consider myself a nacho and margarita expert and when I go out to drink and throw down, I go to cheaper spots that get you drunk. No one should be going to fancy Mexican or Tex-Mex food...ever I judge you based on that, not your service to the country...so perhaps one day, I'll get to debate that with the Secretary, but until then, I'm going to focus back on the story that I was going to tell that you know already.

Secretary Nielsen was eating dinner at the restaurant, which again is too pricey and makes no sense to eat at, when she was approached by a group of protestors yelling about policy that they didn't agree with. They interrupted her dinner to rudely scream at her and her guest as they were trying to have a relaxing evening from what I am sure is one of the highest pressure jobs on the entire planet. After all, she's literally in charge of the first responders and programs that keep our nation safe and knows about far too many threats to human life and our nation in general. She needs a break once in a while, and although I don't agree with her restaurant choice, if it's what makes the person tasked with overseeing the protection our homeland safe feel relaxed, I can deal with it.

The verbal assault and protesting in what I would call her private time was considered to be civil by those who say that we need more civility in the world. How can that be?

How can you say that harassing someone who's not on the playing field is civil? There are so many ways and places to protest policy that you don't agree with, but harassing someone in their private life is another level of low…an actually uncivil level of low.

So what is the playing field and why does it play into the conversation of civility?

In professional baseball, the umpires have an office in every stadium that is typically far away from the players' and management's locker rooms. This office may or may not be too fancy depending on the stadium, but it does have two things in common: a door that can be locked from the inside and a peephole. Why is this?

If you watch baseball, you realize that players and coaches don't always get along with umpires. There are coaches who famously kick dirt, throw bases, turn their caps around, and cuss out umpires based on calls that they made on the playing field.

Early in baseball history, enough umpires got beat up and were threatened after the game that they felt they needed to do a bit more to protect themselves, hence, a special separate office with locked doors and peepholes. After what one team would consider a "bad call," on the playing field, the umpire could essentially take cover off the playing field to protect themselves from athletes who were much larger than them and acted more *uncivil* than they would like to have to deal with.

The playing field in baseball is obvious. It's where the players actually play baseball and follow the rules that are enforced by the umpires. After the nine innings (or however long the game may run) are over, everyone goes to the locker room, showers, gets dressed, and goes home. They don't continue to play the game in the parking lot. They don't continue yelling at the other team or coaches at dinner. And they don't carry around their baseball bats and stay dressed in their uniforms "just in case." They take a break to return to their lives for a bit, then get dressed and play the game the next day against whichever opponent they face.

In politics, the playing field is a little different, but the concept should remain the same. When a politician or appointee is in their office, on the floor of whichever body they represent or need to testify to, at a press conference, rally, or even are on a national television program that they've been asked to be on, they are on the playing field. When they aren't there, they return to their normal lives to relax and take a break. For the most part, being in politics is a lot more stressful than we typically recognize. I say that to also say that there are politicos who don't do anything and live a pretty great life, but for the most part, these folks are hard-working members of political parties who work non-stop and deserve a break.

In a civil society, we would recognize when it's time to fight in politics and when it's time to take a break, but those lines haven't just been blurred by many—they've been flat forgotten or ordered to be ignored.

Maxine Waters made an incredibly uncivil move at a rally by telling her followers to harass Republicans anywhere and everywhere they are. I won't even criticize her in this section of the book for her typical rhetoric of "Impeach 45," which I'm certain at this point she never has the intention of doing. Instead I'll say this, for years, the lines have been hard ones. There is a time to debate and yell at one another, but there is another time to be civil and kind. Waters, in demanding that people harass Republicans, took away those lines in order to encourage people to be complete assholes to one another on *and* off the playing field.

Almost a year ago, I was on a local television show in Washington, D.C. to discuss my experience of being robbed at gunpoint and how I had decided to get my concealed carry permit and purchase a gun to protect myself in the district. In the greenroom with me was Congresswoman Eleanor Holmes Norton, who, similar to Kathleen Sebelius, I have literally no common ground with politically. We recognized each other, knowing full well that we stand on opposite sides of many issues, but had a great conversation about what she was working on and her legitimate concerned about what happened to me.

As we continued to speak, the host of the show dropped in and asked if I told her what I was going to do to protect myself, knowing full well it would get on her nerves. I told her that I was going to seek to obtain a concealed carry permit and own a gun and her response wasn't yelling or getting angry; it was, "Come onnnn; that won't help you." She followed with reasonable debate with me about gun control and what she believed versus what I believed.

We argued for a good five to ten minutes, and then both completed our interviews on air. After the show, we went our separate ways. There was no continuation of the debate; there was no harassment about personal issues; there was no incivility.

I was alone with a United States Congresswoman who argued with me and we were kind and respectful of one another. We also recognized that we were on the playing field where that debate can happen. When it was over, it was over and we both went on about our lives.

That's what civility should be. There should be kindness and respect with one another. No personal attacks, no nude drawings (remember the Women's March), no disgusting comments, and no harassing people at venues where they expect to have privacy and a relaxing night out.

Civility has become a cover and excuse for justifying what Maxine Waters tried to incite. The baseline of a lot of the civility logic is this concept that "I'm civil because I voted for Hillary Clinton, and you're uncivil for voting for Donald Trump." This allows for those who believe themselves to be civil and working for civility to do whatever it takes to accomplish their goals. If that means harassing the Secretary of Homeland Security at a terrible and expensive Mexican restaurant, then so be it, according to them.

Another instance of this "civility" came when protestors attempted to harass Majority Leader Mitch McConnell and his wife, Secretary of the Department of Transportation Elaine Chao. I have to say that this was my favorite of all the terrible videos of harassment to come out and not because of the harassment, but because of the reaction from those who the protestors thought would cower in fear.

That video, where protestors attempted to corner McConnell and his wife while they were exiting a building and getting into an SUV off the playing field shows that Secretary Chao won't be intimidated or harassed. As much as progressives love to pick on weaker, easier targets (we'll get to that in a second) Chao wasn't having any of it. She got in the faces of the protestors rather than run for cover, telling them to leave her and McConnell alone and get lives. It was an incredibly powerful moment watching someone who you wouldn't necessarily believe would take a stand against a group of adult men who were attempting to harass her get right up in their faces.

This brings me to my next point. In civil societies and classier events, we always protect women and children first. I'm not sure why this is a thing. If I'm in trouble somewhere or I'm on a sinking ship, I'm saving myself. Sorry, not sorry...I'm just not prescribing this level of civility. I recall watching the movie *Titanic*, or what little I could stomach of the ridiculously long thing, and seeing that they loaded women and children on to the lifeboats first. Why was this? Because in traditional classy and civil societies, women and children are viewed as weaker and thus given more protection and preference in emergency situations.

I say that to say this: why is it that these "civil" people who call for civility are okay with the harassment of what appears to be mainly women, poor elderly Mitch McConnell, (I'll call him cocaine Mitch somewhere else to balance out this characterization) and Stephen Miller from the Trump administration?

Isn't it odd that those who marched for women's rights in the Women's March and call for civility find it okay to harass women?

We've already discussed Secretary Nielsen, but let's take a moment to cover Sarah Huckabee Sanders. A few months ago, Sarah Sanders and her family decided to go out to a little restaurant called the Red Hen in Lexington, Virginia. I'm not quite sure why she was nearly two hundred miles away from Washington, D.C. trying to go to dinner, but if I had as stressful as a job as she does, I would run far away to relax and do exactly the same.

When she arrived at the restaurant, she was seated, quickly recognized by the staff who called the "civil" owner of the restaurant. The restaurant owner then went out of her way to drive in to the restaurant, come up with a "plan" with her staff, then ask Sanders to leave. This action led to a media firestorm and cheers from many on the left who were overjoyed at the fact that Sarah Sanders was denied service because of her job in politics. Many said that she deserved to be kicked out and not given a chance to relax from her job. And sure, this is completely protected "speech" from the First Amendment, but no one should pretend to call what happened "civil."

If the owner of the Red Hen was being civil, as I'm sure she preaches to others to be, she would have realized that Sarah Sanders wasn't on the playing field and was there to relax in her establishment. Instead, the owner took it upon herself to harass the Sanders family, throwing them out and making a social media spectacle of herself for personal gain.

By any traditional definition of civility, the owner would have allowed Sanders to stay and eat a meal and then speak her mind online later about her disagreement with the White House Press Secretary's stances. But instead, the owner abides by the definition of civility where anyone who supports Donald Trump or worse, works for this president, is some type of lower level of trash that doesn't deserve the respect that those in the bubble have earned by merely being in the bubble.

The cheering on social media and on television encouraging the behavior of the owner of Red Hen and others to "protest" members of the Trump administration would also not be considered "civil" by any traditional sense of the word. Nowhere in modern history other than now has a major political party encouraged the harassment and hatred toward the other party based solely on their politics. It's low, animalistic, and to be completely honest, is a scary set of rules to live by in our modern world.

And sure, this is all protected speech under the First Amendment. That's what the left says in defense of this off the field harassment and they are 100 percent correct. There is nothing in there that says you don't have the right to yell at or get in the faces of politicians anywhere in public, any time you want, because you disagree with them. There are however, common sense standards of morals and civility that have maintained a certain level of logic and respect when it comes to this type of behavior. Blurring what civility actually means, or redefining it as it seems it has been redefined, is where we get in trouble.

When you take away simple, common sense rules like "don't harass politicos at home and when they're not at work," you open our society up to a potential slippery slope of harassment and hatred for political disagreements with anyone, anywhere.

Where then does the line get drawn? When you're finished harassing politicians and that doesn't work, who is the next level of person that you harass? Television hosts? Political pundits? Writers?

Could you imagine if any of this off the field harassment would have happened under the Obama administration? The calls of harassment, racism, and the immediately need to jail protestors would be so loud that you wouldn't be able to hear what anyone else was talking about. But don't worry about that; there's no double standard to see here. Move along, everyone.

While we're here talking about the blurred lines and redefinition of the word civility, can we just take a moment to discuss exactly what it accomplishes to call people names, say disgusting things about them, and harass them in public places and their private dinners and homes?

Nothing.

If you disagree with anything in this book or leave me a bad review, I am going to take action. No longer will I sit and let you tell me I'm not funny, or that my logic doesn't add up, or that the font used in this is too large because I didn't hit a reasonable word limit so we had to increase the size of the font to make it look like I wrote more than just a simple pamphlet. No, I won't stand for it.

I have a few plans in place to civilly protest your dislike of any minor piece of this work.

The first thing I'm going to do is expose all your personal information online. I didn't cover this earlier in the chapter, but doxing, or publishing all your personal information, is a tactic used to "civilly" harass people now. You just simply push all their personal information online and hope that nothing bad happens with it. No big deal. Nothing to see here. Totally reasonable.

After I dox you, I'll probably call your employer and tell them just how terrible you are. If you work at a restaurant, I'll leave bad reviews on the restaurant page, highlighting you and your criticism of me, but with nothing to do with the actual restaurant which I will never visit. These are other tactics that are used by both sides of the aisle. The concept that you don't deserve to be able to make a living because you disagree with me is another completely civil and totally reasonable way that normal human beings deal with each other.

What was that? That didn't work either? Well then, I'll call your spouse's place of business and tell them what you did and how terrible of a human you are. That's happened in the not too distant past. If you disagree with someone's politics or their behavior online, a totally reasonable and civil human being will call up and harass that person's spouse's place of work until their spouse is let go for fear of a public relations nightmare.

Once I ensure that all your personal information is made public and that you and your spouse can no longer provide for your family, then I'll show up to wherever you are in public, whether it be a restaurant, sporting event, whatever it is…or not. I'll just stalk you in public and bring a big crowd of people with signs talking about how terrible you are to shout you down and make sure you know that it was wrong for you to criticize me in any way, shape, or form. Again, this is totally reasonable and civil.

Next, because that's not enough, I'll come to your house with that same crowd, probably when you're asleep late at night, and we'll make noise for days, screaming at you about how terrible it was for you to do what you did. I'll also harass your neighbors while I'm there to make sure that they hate you as well. This is totally reasonable and civil because I say it is.

After publishing your personal information, getting you and your spouse fired from your jobs, then harassing you in public and in private at your house, I think we'll finally see eye to eye and you'll change your opinion on my book and commentary.

What did you say?

That won't change your opinion?

But look at the lengths that I went to to get in your face on multiple occasions, make you lose any source of income, and turn every aspect of your world against you. You can't even sleep anymore. I did all of that to convince you that my work is correct.

No, none of that sounds like fascism or the work of a psychopath *at all*. It's totally reasonable, civil activities driven by freedom of speech. In fact, when we protest you in public or private at your house, we're going to chant "this is what democracy looks like" because this is what I'm saying democracy looks like so that we can influence you to change your mind on the issue of my creativity in this book. Totally reasonable, makes perfect sense, and it's completely civil because I said so.

I went through that exercise, which trust me, can go on much longer to make the point that harassing people will never change their minds on anything at all…ever.

Scaring someone into silence and taking away their ability to live a free and comfortable life merely because they disagree with you is fascism. Calling those fascist actions civil doesn't make you civil…it makes you look like the asshole I talked about at the beginning.

You convince no one to change their mind by publishing their personal information, harassing them, or taking away means to make a living. Sure, you might scare them into hiding, but that's not changing the world; that's not changing hearts and minds; and that's certainly not being civil.

The people who preach that we need to have civility have defined civility not only as their way of life, but also their way of thought. You're not allowed to disagree with them. If you do, they'll go through the absurd lengths of harassment that I mentioned above to try to ruin you.

When children or I fart, we blame someone else first so as to not look like the guilty one. When these protesters and totally reasonable civil human beings harass people, they are the first to point fingers and call that differing opinion fascism. This is no coincidence.

In a world where personal responsibility no longer exists, it's always someone else's fault. That world gets even easier for you when you can simply call yourself a hero or civil and label someone else the villain or uncivil. It justifies your actions, makes you feel like you're doing some sort of good when deep down you know you're not, and it might even get you a few likes and retweets or a bunch of video views online.

Civility in our modern world means anything but what its actual definition is. It's been skewed to give people excuses to justify their actions, attack others, and discriminate against those who with whom they disagree.

CHAPTER 16:

★ ★ ★

WHY TRUMP WON

Racism, misogyny, Russia, Comey, Facebook, Twitter, the Democratic Party, the Republican Party, low information voters, Netflix, WikiLeaks, suburban women, everyone who assumed Hillary would win, Bernie Sanders, *The New York Times,* television executives, content farms in Macedonia, Obama winning two terms, and islamophobia…are only a part of the list of excuses that Hillary Clinton has made for why she lost the election. She'll pull that list out on good days. On the other side of the excuse pile, she and many democratic voters will remind you that she won the popular vote, which she did, by 2,864,974 votes.

The margin of popular votes in a presidential election doesn't matter though, because as you and I know, America is a republic and not a pure democracy and determines the victor of its presidential elections via the Electoral College.

Without digging deeply into the purpose and history of the Electoral College, I can tell you that it was designed to help the different states be adequately represented in the presidential election. The founders predicted and knew from what they had already seen that large clusters of the American population would live in specific areas, like major cities. The concept of the Electoral College was to mimic that of the House of Representatives so that each state would have a representative vote in the presidential election rather than have the election come down to just a few major cities or states determining the election, which would happen in a straight democracy.

This system was devised to prevent an individual from only needing to visit a few specific population-heavy areas to sway the vote and come to power. The term tyrant was tossed around a lot in the creation of the Electoral College…in that they wanted to prevent it. The founders knew how the system could and would be manipulated if there wasn't balance and equal representation brought to it. Crazy how that works isn't it? Because in the occasional news cycle, we hear that Trump is a tyrant because he didn't win the popular election; the founding fathers would disagree.

Let's break down that popular vote that Hillary won. No one seems to ever want to do this. They just say that she won and that the election was stolen. You're going to be surprised at how easily we can account for these numbers when we do. Keep in mind that we're only trying to account for her margin of victory of 2,864,974 votes. Ready? Hold on to something.

In Los Angeles County, aka the City of Los Angeles, Hillary Clinton received 2,464,364 votes as compared to Donald Trump's 769,743. If you're playing along at home, that's a difference of 1,694,621 votes or 59.1 percent of her total margin of popular vote victory, *from just Los Angeles*. Rather than mess around by digging into smaller counties from around the country, let's go straight to the vote totals in Manhattan, just a piece of New York City, shall we?

In Manhattan, a heavily populated part of New York City (in case you needed me to clarify), Hillary Clinton received 579,013 votes compared to Trump's showing of 64,929. This was a difference of 514,084 or 17.9 percent of her entire margin of popular vote victory. So if you're following along with the math here, we have accounted for 77 percent of Hillary Clinton's entire margin of popular vote victory with just Los Angeles and Manhattan. As you can imagine, it's not hard to find the rest of that margin of victory quickly and for that, we'll go to the dead people voting capitol of the United States: Chicago, Illinois.

In 2016, the City of Chicago voted overwhelmingly for Hillary Clinton, 890,705 to Trump's 132,738. This was a difference of

757,967 votes in favor of the first female major party candidate for president and 26.5 percent of her total margin of victory. Are you still following along? If you haven't drifted off like I used to in my math classes in high school, you'd realize that Hillary Clinton's entire margin of popular vote victory (plus a little more) can be accounted for by the vote totals in Los Angeles, Manhattan alone in New York City, and Chicago. Those three cities alone add up to 103.5 percent of her entire margin of victory. That's all it takes.

In fact, you can account for Hillary Clinton's entire margin of victory with basically any combination of the cities of Chicago, San Francisco, Los Angeles, Seattle, Boston, Atlanta, and a few boroughs in New York City. It doesn't take much. Could you imagine if all the country's policies were controlled by just those few population centers? Where they may have a lot of things in common because of their similar trade, population behavior, and business environments, they have nothing in common with a vast majority of the middle of the country, the south, and the states shaped like rectangles up north. The founders of this country knew this when they set up our electoral college system; that's why we have it. It also forces a presidential candidate to go outside of those major cities to reach out and learn about the population's needs. It's a shame Hillary didn't think to campaign in Michigan, Wisconsin, and Pennsylvania; she was busy playing a tyrant's game as the founders would have labeled it. To be fair, they would have probably also laughed at the concept of a woman running for public office, but that was in the 1700s and 1800s and now the idea is something that is within reach.

So why is it that Trump won? What caused it? I know that when we typically discuss this we begin with general election voting results. Hell, I began with general election voting results, but what about the primaries? Donald Trump cut through the "deep bench" of potential Republican nominees like butter to run to an incredible victory...but why was it so easy? The answer: communication.

By 2016, Republicans and Democrats had lost touch on how the world was communicating with one another. By that, I don't mean that they had no idea how to use social media, although if you look at some of the Washington, D.C. based marketing firms and what they claim to be able to do, one could argue that they have no idea how to use social media. I mean clickbait and marketing speak.

One of the pieces I left out of my earlier bio is that I was taught digital marketing by some of the forerunners of the industry; some might call them scammers, but I think what they did was pretty genius. They were able to adapt the news into sales in a way that led a billion dollar a year or more industry of selling knick-knacks to everyone from those who wanted to get rich quick to those who wanted to find love; those who thought the end of the world was coming to those who wanted to lose weight. By the way, that covers the three pillars of digital marketing sales for you in a few more words: health, wealth, and love. The digital marketers I learned from mastered each of the pillars in an incredible fashion, and taught me to do the same. They also taught me how to write the catchy headlines that draw normal, flyover country Americans in to open emails. I say all of that to say this: all of Trump's communication, from Twitter to in person speeches, sounded like this successful digital marketing.

After the first month of his campaign, I knew he was going win, and I went on record in December 2015 to say that he wouldn't just win the primary, but that he would win the whole thing. His messaging is simple and strong, harsh and entertaining, and it makes those who he's trying to reach believe exactly what he's saying. Barack Obama was close to hitting those same notes with "Hope" and "Change" when he first ran, but no one had hit the nail on the head as hard as Trump did with "Make America Great Again," "Lock her up," and "Build that wall." His nicknames of opponents, which he pulled apart one by one still linger today: "Low Energy Jeb!" "Lyin' Ted" "Little Marco." He demeaned them the way a professional wrestler did to such a point that I could be convinced that he got tips from Vincent Kennedy McMahon, the CEO of World Wrestling Entertainment himself. He did appoint McMahon's wife Linda to head the Small Business administration, so perhaps there's something to that.

The magic of the Trump messaging was so strong that what the media and opposition wanted to believe was a joke was getting wall-to-wall coverage on every network. And when the Iowa primary came around, his staff and volunteer "army," which my very close to the campaign sources told me was literally sixty people, pulled off a second-place victory to Ted Cruz's six hundred organized staff and volunteer army. See what I did there dropping the quotes?

Sure, Ted Cruz pulled off Iowa, but with so much more effort—and a lie about Ben Carson dropping out, hence the "Lyin' Ted" moniker. You could see Trump was on to something. From there, it was a cakewalk for the then-candidate. A Lids rush job on a cheap red hat caught on and the systematic picking apart of candidates that would have once been considered locks for the presidency began. Trump connected to the American people. He broke the fourth wall in debates and even if you loathed him, you laughed and cheered when he jabbed at his opponents. There was literally no chance he could have lost the primary unless of course we saw some sort of dramatic team up of Cruz and Rubio, a dual smackdown the likes that we have never seen—at least in recent history—that would have somehow combined their delegate totals. Even then, Trump would have still pulled it off, but it would have at least been a bit more entertainingly close. The general election, however, was a bit of a different story.

And by bit of a different story, I mean that Hillary Clinton's team took a long, hard look at what happened to the Republican candidates that Trump ran over, intensely studying their strategy of pointing out that he had no political experience and was a mean, mouthy guy, then spent millions of dollars and used years of market research on top of it to determine that it was crucial that she do the same exact thing that they did, but with the added bonus that she was a woman. Did you know that she was a *woman*? That was a majority of her campaign: that she was a woman! How could you go wrong with that?

Before we get into just how bad of a stomping Donald Trump gave her in this election, (and I know some of you will say that he didn't win the popular vote, but seriously, who cares at this point? We don't live in a direct democracy so that doesn't count for anything other than maybe a participation certificate) I want to discuss how Hillary Clinton got the nomination and why it was the worst move Democrats could have done to begin with.

Not factoring in the other two or three losers who ran for the Democratic nomination (seriously if you supported Martin O'Malley and weren't paid to do so, you clearly have issues) this was a two-horse race between Bernie Sanders (the socialist) and Hillary Clinton (the representative of the oligarchy).

Unless you lived under a rock for the eight years prior to the 2016 election, you realized that Barack Obama was slowly rolling out more and more socialist policies. Whether it be more social programs that other people would need to pay for, or just good old-fashioned Obamacare, he was trying to turn America into the perfect European Union sister nation. Without doing an in-depth dig, and simply glancing back at my description of the two candidates running for the Democratic nomination, it's easy to see which would have been the perfect successor to this legacy: the one who of course would have continued down the road of socialist policies.

Bernie, was the closest representation of the Democratic base at the time that the 2016 presidential race came along; unfortunately, it wasn't his time. With all the talk of rigged elections, the super delegate system that the DNC had in place ensured that no matter how popular the elderly Sanders got, he was *never* going to win.

And boy did he get popular.

Near the end of the primary election cycle for the Democrats, Bernie had been packing out stadiums, colleges and just about any event he spoke at. He was turning crowds of young people the likes of which only Barack Obama had seen the first time he ran for office and the size of which only Donald Trump was getting during the Republican primary cycle on the other side of the aisle.

One would think that a political party would obviously be in favor of choosing anyone who filled stadiums of people to be their nominee, right? I mean superficially looking at people turning out in droves for Bernie would be more than enough for that to convince the DNC overlords to give him the nod...no? Well then certainly Hillary Clinton was turning her own huge crowds during that same time period.

The problem was that she wasn't.

There were multiple stories of Clinton events that barely turned out two hundred people. Her stops at state fairs and school gymnasiums were so weakly attended that camera angles were thrown in to make the crowds seem larger. To add insult to injury, Clinton was known for showing up to events forty-five minutes to two hours late. She didn't even show that she cares about those few people who were coming out to see her.

So the DNC took a look at a charismatic man in Bernie Sanders who was a continuation and progression of Barack Obama's policy legacy, and who was also filling stadiums full of energetic young people, *and* who was winning primary votes at a rate that no one expected him to...and they chose to use their loaded super delegate system to stomp out his drive and put Hillary Clinton on her pre-determined pedestal.

Somehow it was her time. Perhaps she lucked out that Joe Biden didn't run. He was charismatic and the perfect continuation of Obama's policies, but due to tragic personal reasons, he took time off for the first time in his eternal political career.

Hillary Clinton was handed a win that she really didn't earn other than happening to wait around for a long enough period that she somehow deserved it.

Side note: I was on a terrible first date seven months after the election of President Trump, and the woman started talking about politics. It was D.C., so it's nearly impossible to escape talking about politics on a first date. Obviously again because it's Washington, D.C., she was a huge progressive who hated every second that Donald Trump had been in office.

The date was fine until she brought up the election and without revealing my political beliefs, I told her that I thought Bernie would have had a much stronger chance at defeating Trump than

Hillary, citing everything that I mentioned above. How did this adult woman react?

She began sobbing at the bar. Sobbing. At. The. Bar.

In public.

With people around.

The bartender and the woman next to her jumped to her aid, as if I had done something to cause her to cry. What happened next will shock you.... Yes, I use clickbait lines in this book—why not?

When the other patrons and bartenders asked what was wrong, she said "Tell them! Tell them what you said about Bernie possibly winning!"

And so I proceeded to discuss exactly what I said above about how the system had been rigged against him and that it was only logical that he should have been given the opportunity to bring his stadiums full of socialism to the mainstream for people to decide between he and Trump; their reaction seven months after the election?!

They all also began to cry.

All of them.

The entire bar was crying about the election of Donald Trump on my first date.

One person thanked me for "speaking the truth...because it needed to be heard." They were all progressives, they all loathed Hillary, and they all cried that Bernie wasn't the democratic nominee because he could have had a reasonable chance against Trump when they knew Hillary would be defeated.

That was one of the worst/best first dates I've ever been on. There wasn't a second date, even though she thought that we were cool after she starting crying and motivating the bar to cry along with her, but damn did I get a good story out of it. So if you're reading this, woman from Bumble who embarrassed herself and looked like an adult baby at a bar on a first date, thank you.

Also, while we're here, if you're still crying about the results of the 2016 election now, or seven months after, or even that night, you really need to re-evaluate your life. Politics is politics and typically balances out after a while. You had eight years of policy and politicians that you loved; now the other team gets their chance because that politician didn't do a good enough job to keep his team in power after his time was up. That's all it is. Get over it. Be adults. Move on. You look pathetic, especially in public on a first date with a guy who's now writing a book about how pathetic you look.

So where were we? Oh yes. Hillary Clinton ran the exact same campaign against Trump that every losing Republican ran in their primary against the man, adding only that she's a woman, and expected to win. I don't know how she, let alone anyone else on her billion dollar-plus campaign, didn't see the end results coming.

So why did Trump win?

Certainly Hillary Clinton being the altogether wrong pick for the Democrats and moving forward with the same strategy of campaign as the other Republican losers are two factors, but what *really* did it?

It was the mythical silent majority.

In one of Dave Chappelle's newish Netflix specials, Chappelle discusses what it was like to go to the polls to vote for Barack Obama in 2008 versus what it was like to vote for Donald Trump in 2016.

The difference in the elections and disappointment in Trump winning can be summarized by his line on poor white people: "I've never had a problem with white people ever in my life. But, full disclosure; the poor whites are my least favorites. We've got a lot of trouble out of them."

In 2008 when he went to vote for who would eventually become the first black president of the United States, he describes having to wait in line with poorer black people. The line was long, it took forever to vote, but he knew upon showing up to the polls that something was different, that change was upon us, and that Barack Obama was going to win.

He knew the same when he showed up to the polls in 2016…except instead of poorer black people at the polls, it was a line around the block of poor white people. He knew as soon as he saw the lines that Hillary Clinton's campaign was dead in the water and that all the polls and pundits saying that she was going to win were wrong.

The poor white people are what has been known by many as the silent majority in the country. If you're reading this in flyover, I'm probably talking about you. You're the group of people that are often ignored by the Hollywood, media, and mainstream bubbles that so many people live in. You're the folks that are more than likely living paycheck to paycheck, trying to figure out how to pay your bills, and trying to find a way to make sure you get your kids to college so that they can have a life better than your own. How do I know that? Because that was my family growing up.

Politics don't really concern you. Stormy Daniels, Russian collusion, and other stories that rally the bubble and Twitter don't matter in your world and they shouldn't. You've got better things to deal with; you've got bigger things to deal with.

Looking back on a world that as a child I never understood, I see that my family struggled many days to make sure we had food to eat and I had clean clothes to wear to school. I remember once complaining to my mom in elementary school that I had had a peanut butter and jelly sandwich every day for lunch for two months and I wanted to mix it up. I didn't realize until adulthood what a challenge it posed for her and my dad to shift their budget to afford to send me to school with something else. They pulled it off though. There were times looking back that church people would stop by with casseroles or chicken—cool different things to eat than what I was used to—not for the sake of variety or a potluck. As an adult, I realized this was done because we didn't have money to keep our refrigerator stocked because my father was out of work.

If my parents would have been posed with a question about a social issue, their response would have been the same as many of yours: "we don't care." And surely if they don't care about a social issue, that's the last thing that's going to get them out to the polls.

What would get them out to the poles? Hope. Hope for a better tomorrow and a chance to have a better crack at getting food on the table. Hope for a little bit more money back in their paychecks so that they wouldn't have to give away their hard-earned money to the federal government. And knowing that they really couldn't improve upon their job situation, that they were stuck with whatever jobs they could find, hope that their son would have a better chance at life than they did.

Obama promised this hope and change in 2008 and it never came for those people in the middle of the country, for the silent majority. Hell, it never came for the poor black people that voted for him either. Further, the change and improvement of lives never came the eight years before Obama under George W. Bush. So in 2016, America didn't look to political party for hope; they looked for a radical outsider to make the change.

And that radical outsider, as much as you may or may not agree, was Donald Trump.

He wasn't a part of the political system or in the swamp. He was a mouthy billionaire playboy who had nothing to lose in stating his opinion and had, before announcing that he was going to run for president, won the respect and admiration of most of the population. Even when he would do something ridiculous like pick a fight with Rosie O'Donnell, he was applauded by America. There were no calls of misogyny or sexism. No. Instead, they would laugh along with him. He was America's favorite troll—again, until he announced that he was seriously running for president.

Even documentarian and noted meatball sub lover Michael Moore knew Trump would win. In a documentary he did on the candidate, albeit ultimately to say that he would deceive his voters and be terrible for the country, Moore identified Trump as the "F-you" or the "Molotov cocktail" to the system in the 2016 election, and showed, in dramatic fashion, that he would pull through.

Everything I've said so far isn't enough to convince everyone to have gotten out to vote for Trump. Sure, there was a poor candidate with a poor campaign in Hillary and sure, there was this buck to the system that was needed that came along with the potential to finally have the hope and change that had been promised but never delivered, but there was one more factor: the mouthy progressive left.

To those on the left who might be hate reading this book or are looking for excuses to be angry, you might want to go to the mirror right now, look in it, and get ready to point fingers at one of the biggest factors as to why Donald Trump became the 45th president of the United States: you.

Remember that silent majority that I was talking about, the people who I'm familiar with because they literally were my family growing up? Those folks that were looking for better options to bring that hope and change to their lives—why again? Because they were never sure or were highly in doubt in a paycheck-to-paycheck world where their next meal may come from.

What happens if you ask those people in regular conversation, not a formal polling situation, about a social issue like gay marriage or trans bathroom use or pay differences between men and women? They typically respond honestly with, "I don't care."

And they don't care. Why? Because unless it directly touches their lives or deals with their income, they don't have the time or energy to be concerned with it.

Here's where the mouthy progressive left *really* got them to vote for Trump. It's fun to name-call, isn't it? It's fun to pretend that you have enemies and that you're morally superior to those with whom you disagree. When those in the silent majority were posed questions about things that they literally didn't care about, your response to them, ya mouthy leftists, was to call them in no particular order: racist, homophobic, sexist, misogynist, islamophobic, xenophobic, bigoted, and whatever other title you could pull out of your hat to call them.

Hillary made it even easier and extra convenient for you to name-call by lumping that pile of names into the "basket of deplorables."

By the way, those social issues that we're talking about here? They're first world problems. They are the problems that we should have when everyone is happy, healthy, safe, and living their best life attaining the American dream. A biological man believing and having the means to dress and identify as a woman having access to optional clean public restrooms and making the choice to go into one that he previously wouldn't qualify to enter because of his biological sex *is a first world problem.*

The silent majority? They don't care about your first world problems because they still have third and second world problems. Third world problems include having reasonable and clean housing as well as being able to put food on the table regularly. Second world problems include having the ability to get access to proper education for their kids.

Spoiler alert: people who have third and second world problems don't even remotely care about your first world problems; they have deeper issues to face.

So let's take all of that information and put it into a nifty package for review. Follow along.

You've been promised hope and change for a generation or more by both a charismatic Republican in George W. Bush and a charismatic Democrat who literally used "hope" and "change" as a campaign slogan and neither delivered. You're now left looking for actual hope and change and you're face with the choice of Hillary Clinton, who represents the swamp (or the establishment) versus the mouthy billionaire who looks like an outsider and essentially gives the middle finger to whoever he doesn't like. Couple that with Hillary's campaign running on major social issues, which were first world problems when the silent majority still has third world problems. Then add that people with second and third world problems don't care about first world issues and stir in the insult that progressives call these folks a variety of not-so-creative names for daring to not care about these first world issues. Suddenly, you've awakened a sleeping giant and made them feel damn-near forced to have to vote for Donald Trump for their very survival.

For the cherry on top, there is the comment from Hillary Clinton that, "We're going to put a lot of coal miners and coal companies out of business."

There is not one person that I know who lives in flyover country that doesn't know someone who was related to or directly in the coal industry. When she said that, she was speaking directly to everyone in that silent majority who understood the third world struggle of providing food on a regular basis for a family, and telling them that she would make their lives worse, stomping out an industry that has provided for so many friends of friends and family members in a part of the country that she clearly has no understanding of.

In one simple gloating sentence, Hillary Clinton stared right into the heart of one of the largest voting blocks in the nation and declared the end of not their way of life, but the very way that they are able to have the means to live. Her campaign should have been pronounced dead at that point, but it wasn't. Why?

Because the billionaire came with tons of entertaining baggage.

You can't live the life of a literal billionaire playboy who was on the cover of *Playboy* magazine and not have some sort of garbage in your past. From exes to statements, Donald Trump did nothing more than live the life that he worked and was entitled to live, and the political system thought they could use it against him.

Hillary had no strategy to beat Trump other than say that he was nasty and said mean things, the same as every other candidate who lost to him in the past had said. And she had gaffed so much and was flailing but never realized it because her fans in the media believed in her like they did as children that Santa Claus provided presents for them on Christmas.

From their perches in the bubble, it was hard to see down into the rest of the country, to see the pain and struggle of middle America. After all, they're the civil ones who go to fancy restaurants and celebrate themselves like they do something other than watch C-span and come up with groan-worthy quips and three-paragraph articles about tweets.

They thought the world would be as offended by Trump as they pretended to be, clutching their pearls and gasping with repulsion every time he would get a crowd of deplorables to cheer "Lock her up" or "Build that wall" or "Fake News." And it's easy to see why they would believe in themselves because they get lots of attention from their colleagues and those they want to impress in the bubble with their sad attempts at one-liners on Twitter and in front of cameras on news television shows that are barely watched by anyone outside of their bubble.

They had no concept of what was going on and that the silent majority had been infuriated and pushed to Trump while they were busy at the most ridiculously priced happy hours in the nation. Seriously, I went to this place in West Virginia once where you could get a double shot of Wild Turkey 101 and a beer for three dollars and fifty cents during happy hour. In D.C., that would run you ten to thirteen dollars.

The media was as out of touch as the campaign they admired with Hillary, and so no one caught on to the movement that happened. And no one saw it coming.

Trump won because he was different.

Trump won because Hillary presented no argument that could beat his being different.

Trump won because the hope and change he promised seemed like a different hope and change than what had been presented over the past decade.

Trump won because while Hillary pushed first world issues, he spoke to the third world issues this country has.

Trump won because those who didn't care about first world issues were called names.

Trump won because Hillary directly offended an industry that touches nearly everyone that doesn't live in a bubble.

Trump won because in the middle of their circle jerk about their bubble-selves, the media didn't know understand the change that was happening in the rest of the country.

Trump won and some of you still can't wrap your heads around that very simple concept let alone the fact that you don't understand the third world level struggle that so many in this country face on a daily basis.

At this rate, he's going to keep winning all the way through the 2020 election too because Democrats have no new strategy to beat him.

★ ★ ★

A CONCLUSION BECAUSE AT THE BEGINNING WE HAD AN INTRO, SO THAT MEANS THERE'S GOING TO BE SOME SORT OF CONCLUSION

In an ideal world, everyone should have the ability to run cleanly on their record and have an equal crack at getting their party elected. Voters should have the opportunity to learn about candidates and their platforms freely and have the information given to them so that they all make informed decisions rather than choosing based on a thirty-second commercial, a guy holding a sign, or maybe even just the sign without a guy. People on both sides should be honest and work with one another to compromise, keeping in mind that this country won't succeed unless we all hold hands, hug on a regular basis, and do a bunch of lame stuff. Okay. That's enough; I got sick of writing all that idealistic crap.

It isn't an ideal world. Things aren't perfect. Near the beginning of the book, I gave you my favorite line of political theory from James Madison's *Federalist 51*. I want to give you an entire passage now so that you understand that we'll just never get along.

"But the great security against a gradual concentration of the several powers in the same department, consists in giving to those

who administer each department the necessary constitutional means and personal motives to resist encroachments of the others. The provision for defense must in this, as in all other cases, be made commensurate to the danger of attack. Ambition must be made to counteract ambition. The interest of the man must be connected with the constitutional rights of the place. It may be a reflection on human nature, that such devices should be necessary to control the abuses of government. But what is government itself, but the greatest of all reflections on human nature? If men were angels, no government would be necessary. If angels were to govern men, neither external nor internal controls on government would be necessary. In framing a government which is to be administered by men over men, the great difficulty lies in this: you must first enable the government to control the governed; and in the next place oblige it to control itself. A dependence on the people is, no doubt, the primary control on the government; but experience has taught mankind the necessity of auxiliary precautions."

There are so many lines that hold true in this passage. Men aren't angels and will continue to fight with one another because of their own egos and ambitions. I'm taking this passage a bit out of context because it applies to both the actual checks and balances in the government and those that surround the government. This entire book has focused on those that surround it. If we talked more about what was going on inside, I'd have bored you to death even more.

Madison had it right that at the end of the day, political people will want more and more power and that will in essence keep opposing sides at bay. So as much as we all hate to admit it, as long as both parties keep fighting, we may not live in an ideal world, but we live in more of a framer's ideological world. Maybe it's just the way it's supposed to be.

You know, a lot of times when people write books, they get this false sense of accomplishment that they're somehow smarter than other people. That's not what this thing has been about. I already have a healthy ego.

I could've done a lot of things to gain more respect here, but each of them would be playing a character that I'm not. could've labeled myself a journalist, I could've pulled out bigger words and written more formally, and I could've certainly seemed more prophetic instead of condescending in the way that I describe things, but that would be a complete waste of everyone's time, and would've been pretty solidly run-of-the-mill and boring.

My goals here are simple: I want the world to be better. I want America to be better first. And in order to America to be better, we all need to be better, even the man in the mirror. That was so dramatic, wasn't it? I hit a very dramatic Michael Jackson reference there. Cue the music.

I point out flaws, I call people stupid, and I expose hypocrisy because I hope that in the middle of some sort of snarky comment and someone retorting by calling me a jerk or an asshole, that they think about what I said and take it to heart.

One of my favorite progressive friends once told me that what sets me apart from a lot of critics that he would listen to is that he knew without a doubt that I loved this country and the people in it. I took that to heart. Also, that guy stopped talking to me because one day I told him hypothetically that I'd probably consider working for the Koch brothers if they ever offered me a job. Ihaven't heard from him since.

He also at one point two years ago had more Twitter followers than me, but since catching Trump Derangement Syndrome, he stopped being incredibly funny and started tweeting non-stop about hating Trump. He's gained maybe five hundred followers in that time. Sad!

There we go. I wouldn't have felt right concluding the book without taking a shot at someone who may or may not exist due to legal reasons.

I'll leave you with this thought. Don't be an idiot like that loser who clearly at one point had good thoughts, but then lost his mind over politics, and who also may or may not have existed in real life.

Oh and also don't be like those people at the protest at the beginning, or people who believe in crazy conspiracy theories, or people who don't take personal responsibility, or liars who make fake news, or pretentious assholes who scream about civility, or anybody else who I didn't like in this book, or people who didn't like this book.

Dear person who bought my book:

I can't thank you enough for buying my book, so in my gratitude for doing so, I'd like to offer you something that will not only change your life, but also save you time walking through the downtown area of most metropolitan cities, especially in Washington, D.C. These are the tips and tricks that I have learned to help avoid those poor interns whose entire job it is to get you to sign a petition or donate to a charity.

Feel free to remove this section from the book to keep it handy in your pocket or purse to know exactly what to do when you know you can't avoid them on your commute down the sidewalk.

And keep in mind that even though these methods have been tailored here to avoid petition-getting interns, they can be applied to just about any scenario where you'd like to avoid people.

—Tim
P.S.—I love you.

★ ★ ★

BONUS: THE OFFICIAL MANUAL OF HOW TO AVOID HAVING TO SIGN A PETITION OR HEAR A FUNDRAISING PITCH FOR SOMETHING YOU HAVE NO INTEREST IN

Welcome to the The Official Manual of How to Avoid Having to Sign a Petition or Hear a Fundraising Pitch for Something You Have No Interest In!

In most major cities on just about any day of the week, there are dozens upon dozens of people crowding the sidewalks with something for you to sign or something for you to donate to. They're aggressive—annoyingly aggressive—and spoiler alert, you probably don't have the time to speak with them, any interest in their issue, or the money to spend on the charity.

If you live in the middle of the country, you may not experience this, but keep it handy if you ever vacation in a "bubble area" where this might happen. ou're probably too nice of a person and naïve to the aggression of the intern sent out to get whatever their goal is to get from you on the street. Your natural reaction will be to stop and speak with them. Don't. Follow what I've written here and avoid losing any "me-time" on your vacation.

This simple guide is my gift to you for reading my book so that you can escape the clutches of these not-necessarily-evil people who just want your time, authorization and money.

There are two major strategies to avoid having to deal with a petition-getting intern:

1. **Ignore them altogether.**

2. **Engage them in an appropriately ignorant way.**

STRATEGY 1: IGNORING THE PETITION GETTER

The best and easiest way to get past someone trying to get you to sign a petition is to completely ignore them. In theory, this is very easy to do, but in practice, it's nearly impossible because of social norms. We weren't trained to ignore people when they approach us and say, "Can I have a minute of your time?" or "Can I ask you a question?" So ignoring can be tough. The real trick here is to make it difficult or nearly impossible for them to speak to you. This can be accomplished very simply with the right props.

1: THE CELL PHONE METHOD

What you do here is stare at your cell phone and act like you're doing something on it. If it looks like you're merely reading texts, people feel like they can still talk to you, but if you're dialing or actively texting, they won't bother you. That would be awkward for them, right?

The second and more obvious use of the cell phone in this method is to act like you're talking on it. Let's face it, no one actually talks on a cell phone anymore, so it's going to take time to learn how to fake a conversation with the phone being held to your ear. When you hold it, say a few things like "mmhmmm" or "I totally agree."

If you're feeling particularly creative that day, feel free to talk about a recently deceased relative in order to make them feel guilty for even thinking about attempting to approach you, or yell "Sell

sell sell," which is what all important businessmen do when they're on their cellphones.

The final and most complex way to avoid someone trying to hustle you on the street is to pretend to be taking a selfie. Sure, you may be in a completely uninteresting part of town, but get creative and pretend that you're a tourist who has never seen a Starbucks before or that the street sign is your last name! Another option with selfie avoidance is good old-fashioned self-love. You know what you need to do just as someone asked you if you liked keeping kids alive? Check yourself out. You never know when your hair could be out of place, and right then and there is the time to make sure it's perfect.

2: THE HEADPHONES METHOD

This is much easier than the previous method of avoidance. It requires *visible* headphones being plugged into your ears. All you have to do is pretend that you're listening to something awesome. If they start to lunge for you like rude people would, simply point to your ears as if you're listening to something better than hearing an intern's pitch to sign a petition. And let's face it, listening to nothing is better than listening to the intern's pitch to sign a petition. Keep in mind what I said here: the headphones have to be visible. No earbuds or else you risk them trying to hustle you more. There has to be an attached wire and something of a color that stands out from your clothing choice.

3: THE SUNGLASSES METHOD

Just wear sunglasses and act like you don't see them. The key here is to convince yourself that no one can see you when you have sunglasses on. Don't act out, just maintain a straight path as if you are invisible while wearing the sunglasses.

If you aren't comfortable with that, add a white cane and pretend that you're blind. No one's going to pitch signing a petition or donating to a charity to blind people. Not that there's anything wrong with blind people, but interns won't know how to approach or pitch to them and they'll be befuddled by how they would have a blind person sign the petition. It's too complex of an ordeal for them, so they'll avoid it.

4: THE TALK TO A FRIEND METHOD

The best way to pass the interns on the street is by being in a conversation with someone already. It is absolutely too awkward for an intern to attempt to break into another person's conversation and try to pitch whatever you've got to pitch. Trust me. This one works 99.9 percent of the time. If you're heterosexual and walking with your boyfriend or girlfriend and the intern's opening line is "what a beautiful couple," simply act offended and say something like "Sorry, we're gay."

5: THE READING SOMETHING METHOD

You don't actually have to be able to read to practice this avoidance technique. Just have a book or printed publication in your hands and act like you're reading it. First of all, people will be confused as to what's going on while you're reading the book, because people no longer buy printed books other than this one. Secondly, no one is going to interrupt you while you're focused on something else.

Just a quick warning with this method: the larger the item blocking your line of sight, the better chance that you'll have of a trip and fall encounter where the intern will help you up and then proceed to get you to sign their petition. So whatever you do, don't use a full open newspaper. Stick to novels, folded newspapers and other printed material.

Note: a kindle, iPad, or other e-reader are also acceptable to use, just make sure that you are staring intently at the screen as if it's the most important thing you've ever read in your life.

Second Note: if you couple this method with the one where you pretend to be blind, no one will talk to you on the street ever. A 100 percent probability of success.

STRATEGY 2: ENGAGE THEM IN AN APPROPRIATELY IGNORANT WAY.

This strategy is much more fun if you're a jerk, but it takes a bit of preparation. It sometimes requires that you know the subject matter so that you can make the appropriate ridiculous comment in order to avoid it.

Typically, petition getting interns are promoting one of these five following organizations or subject matters:

1. Planned Parenthood

2. Some children's fund thing.

3. Something about oceans

4. Giving to women in third world countries.

5. Planned Parenthood again (Seriously, forget what they do for a moment. They are the worst when it comes to harassing people on the streets. Maybe take a break from planning everyone's parenthood and plan your budget so you don't have to annoy so many people on the streets.)

It's important to note that with each of these engaging scenarios, you're going to want to keep moving. The goal here is dismissiveness and brevity. So do not stop for any reason, unless otherwise noted below.

1: THE I HATE (BLANK) METHOD

This almost never fails. Figure out what subject they are going to speak about and fill in the blank appropriately. If it's Planned Parenthood, "I hate parents," will work. If it's the children's fund thing, say "I hate children." You get the idea.

If the subject matter is oceans, feel free to pick any sea creature and hate on it. This will also prove to be successful.

Whatever you do, don't say something that will engage them. Please note that I said, "I hate parents," for Planned Parenthood and not "I hate abortions." The "parents" statement doesn't really make sense, so it's dismissive. The "abortions" statement will elicit a reaction from the interns where they will want to discuss what Planned Parenthood does and give you statistics. If you fall into that trap, you lose. Say something dismissive to start with and move on.

2: THE I ALREADY GIVE TO YOU GUYS ~~LIE~~ METHOD

I never recommend lying. It ranks as the second-lowest of the low-brow ways to avoid the interns (pretending to be blind is the worst) and in most religions, it's a sin. All you have to do here is say, "I already give to you." They will reply with a "Oh, okay, thanks!" and you'll be on your way. They might even high five you. You will take that high five and walk away with the guilt of knowing you influenced someone to high five you because of a lie.

The error here would be to say, "I *think* I already give to you." The word "think" will appear to be a question to the petition getting intern who will then attempt to engage you to make sure that you're either definitely giving to them or will give to them. What you're doing here by adding the word "think" is identifying yourself as someone who gives to charity, which makes them smell blood in the water like a shark. They might even have the ability to look up in their system to confirm that you give to them; you're dead in the water at that point.

3: THE I HAVE TO GET TO SOMETHING (MORE IMPORTANT THAN YOU) METHOD

This method is the most common amongst businesspeople. What you want to do here is walk briskly and with purpose. You will automatically seem more important and like a valuable contributor to society even though most of us know that you aren't.

An intern can't argue with your more important schedule than theirs. After all, if they were important, they wouldn't be out there collecting signatures or fundraising. Oh that was too mean of me. I take it back, but won't delete it from this manual. You'll begin to get annoyed by these people enough that you'll think mean things like that when you walk by them. Better you hear it here first so you don't feel guilty when it's in your head.

4: THE ANY RIDICULOUS STATEMENT METHOD

In this method, you can just say anything ridiculous that you would like. Incomplete sentences, insane sounding phrases, and statements about your favorite pet are just a few suggestions. Anything that you say that is completely out of place really works here. Just make sure that you direct the statement at the petition getting intern.

A few examples are:

- "My mom just told me that cats are great."

- "The building back there looks like cheese."

- "I just saw the craziest toe configurations."

Be creative with this. Don't just use these lines—make up something on your own. Just make sure that it doesn't involve anything to do with them. The key is to not engage *with* them here, but rather to engage *at* them.

5: THE I M NOT INTERESTED METHOD

What's wrong with you? Are you boring and honest? Don't ever use this method. They get that all day long. Be creative.

6: THE ULTIMATE METHOD

Keep in mind that nineteen out of twenty of these petitions are from left-leaning organizations, so simply say, "I'm a Republican."

In the end, the key is to not engage the petition getting interns; it will waste your time, their time, or both. You aren't going to convince them that their organization is wrong; they're in the field in terrible conditions working for them—it's just not going to happen.

Have fun, be safe out there, and if you ever actually get the urge to donate to something while out walking on the street, just Venmo or Paypal me instead.

ABOUT THE AUTHOR

Tim Young is a hilarious comedian who's made a career with his biting take on politics and media.